Music and Liturgy,
Identity and Formation

American Society of Missiology
Monograph Series

Chair of Series Editorial Committee, James R. Krabill

The ASM Monograph Series provides a forum for publishing quality dissertations and studies in the field of missiology. Collaborating with Pickwick Publications—a division of Wipf and Stock Publishers of Eugene, Oregon—the American Society of Missiology selects high quality dissertations and other monographic studies that offer research materials in mission studies for scholars, mission and church leaders, and the academic community at large. The ASM seeks scholarly work for publication in the series that throws light on issues confronting Christian world mission in its cultural, social, historical, biblical, and theological dimensions.

Missiology is an academic field that brings together scholars whose professional training ranges from doctoral-level preparation in areas such as Scripture, history and sociology of religions, anthropology, theology, international relations, interreligious interchange, mission history, inculturation, and church law. The American Society of Missiology, which sponsors this series, is an ecumenical body drawing members from Independent and Ecumenical Protestant, Catholic, Orthodox, and other traditions. Members of the ASM are united by their commitment to reflect on and do scholarly work relating to both mission history and the present-day mission of the church. The ASM Monograph Series aims to publish works of exceptional merit on specialized topics, with particular attention given to work by younger scholars, the dissemination and publication of which is difficult under the economic pressures of standard publishing models.

Persons seeking information about the ASM or the guidelines for having their dissertations considered for publication in the ASM Monograph Series should consult the Society's website—www.asmweb.org.

Members of the ASM Monograph Committee who approved this book are:

Paul V. Kollman, Associate Professor of Theology and Executive Director Center for Social Concerns (CSC), University of Notre Dame

Robert Gallagher, Chair of the Intercultural Studies department and Director of M.A. (Intercultural Studies), Wheaton College Graduate School

Music and Liturgy, Identity and Formation

A Study of Inculturation in Turkey

SUE WHITTAKER

FOREWORD BY
ROBERTA R. KING

American Society of Missiology Scholarly Monograph Series 56

☙PICKWICK *Publications* · Eugene, Oregon

MUSIC AND LITURGY, IDENTITY AND FORMATION
A Study of Inculturation in Turkey

American Society of Missiology Scholarly Monograph Series 56

Pickwick Publications
An Imprint of Wipf and Stock Publishers
199 W. 8th Ave., Suite 3
Eugene, OR 97401

www.wipfandstock.com

PAPERBACK ISBN: 978-1-7252-9724-1
HARDCOVER ISBN: 978-1-7252-9725-8
EBOOK ISBN: 978-1-7252-9726-5

Cataloguing-in-Publication data:

Names: Whittaker, Sue, author. | King, Roberta R., foreword.

Title: Music and liturgy, identity and formation : a study of inculturation in Turkey / by Sue Whittaker ; foreword by Roberta R. King.

Description: Eugene, OR: Pickwick Publications, 2021 | American Society of Missiology Scholarly Monograph Series 56 | Includes bibliographical references and index.

Identifiers: ISBN 978-1-7252-9724-1 (paperback) | ISBN 978-1-7252-9725-8 (hardcover) | ISBN 978-1-7252-9726-5 (ebook)

Subjects: LCSH: Hymns, Turkey. | Christianity and culture. | Music—Turkey—Religious aspects—Christianity. | Identification (Religion)—Political aspects—Turkey.

Classification: ML345.T85 W55 2021 (print) | ML345.T85 (ebook)

08/19/21

To Pastor Turgay and Sibel Üçal,
and my brothers and sisters in Christ
at All Saints Moda in Istanbul, Turkey

Contents

Contents

Part III: Praying Twice: Modes and Means

Tables

Figures

Maps

Photographs

Pronunciation Guide

THE TURKISH ALPHABET HAS six letters that have no equivalent character in the Latin alphabet—the consonants ç, ş, and ğ and the vowels ö, ü, and ı. On the other hand, c, o, and u do have an equivalent character, but they differ phonetically from those in the English language.

ç/Ç   as in *ch*irp

ş/Ş   as in *sh*un

ğ/Ğ   A soundless letter. It lengthens the preceding vowel.

a/A   as the "a" in c*a*r

e   Sounds like the "a" in play

i/İ   Dotted i, as the double "e" sound in m*ee*t.

ı/I   Undotted ı, has an "uh" sound

O   as the "o" in *o*pen

ö   as the "ur" in b*ur*n (approximate)

u   as the "oo" in b*oo*t

ü/Ü   as the "u" in ref*u*se

Foreword

SOUNDSCAPES MATTER! FROM BUZZING ferry boats crossing the waterways of Istanbul, Turkey, to the mélange of diverse calls of the minarets strewn through-out this world class city, the sounds of daily life create an ambience of dynamic interaction, including those of people at worship. One wonders; what in the world is God doing through music and liturgy in a country that has historically played such a critical role in World Christianity, yet is now Islamic? What are the implications?

I have spent a lifetime pursuing the contextualization of the Gospel for making Christ known and worshipped through cultural musics and the arts. Although I have led worship in urban African settings, the majority of my research has taken place mainly in rural Africa. This was due to a missiological need to understand local and indigenous contexts, and only then to stimulate contextualization as an outsider. With the growing movements of studying the intersections of culture and worship, i.e. "ethnodoxology," comes the critical need to move further into urban settings such as world-class contexts with their myriads of overlapping cultural frames. Additionally, the inculturation of liturgies in the midst of a nation dominated by a world faith such as Islam raises another critical need in today's global world. Dr. Whittaker's study on a Turkish musical insider, Pastor Turgay Üçal, addresses these critical questions head on.

In today's fragmented world, it is truly rare to see a local pastor take up the mantle to compose worship songs that profoundly speak into a church's unique context. Thus, this investigation of an insider doing inculturation through local music and the arts raises to the surface profound insights that would take more than a lifetime for outsiders to learn. In Dr. Whittaker's excellent and fully-orbed research—from interviewing the pastor-cum-composer, family, congregants, and Protestant church leaders, plus musicological study of the lyrics and cultural musical practices, we are gifted with a model that guides us through key questions that can help to inform the church worldwide how to worship and witness with impact and theological depth. If you are interested in pursuing spiritual formation that is transformative in becoming more like Christ, I wholeheartedly invite you to join in the journey.

Roberta R. King, PhD

Professor of Communication and Ethnomusicology
Fuller Theological Seminary
August 19, 2020

Acknowledgments

ALL SAINTS MODA (ASM) is a place where I can see "the future that awaits us,"[1] thanks to all those who offered me their support and encouragement. My first debt of gratitude is to Pastor Turgay Üçal and the local assembly: the subjects of this project, who willingly gave of their time and friendship and who taught me so much. I am likewise indebted to those working within the greater Protestant community: the pastors, worship leaders, missionaries, academics, and others who helped me to find my way in a new field. Special thanks to the ASM office assistants, Jaklin and Ani, for their warm hospitality and the bottomless cups of hot tea (with sweets) they served during my many interviews with Turgay.

Mentors, colleagues, and friends have accompanied me on this journey from the beginning. My heartfelt appreciation goes to my dissertation director and advisor, Dr. Roberta King, who guided this project from the initial research stage to completion. She helped bring clarity to my thinking and writing, and her patience to follow my pace allowed me to undertake critical new directions in later revisions. She has been an inspiration to me. I also am grateful to Sherwood and Judith Lingenfelter for leading our cohort group with knowledge, experience, and spiritual wisdom. Others include my wonderful colleagues Lila Balisky, Amelia Koh-Butler, and Megan Meyers, with whom I shared all the joys and challenges of the doctoral process. I learned from each of them.

I offer my appreciation to Jayson Knox of the International Turkey Network (ITN), who in 2007 invited me to sift through his fifteen-year

---

1. Chupungco, "Liturgical Inculturation."

xix

collection of cassette tapes and CDs as a first step to understanding the state of worship music in the Protestant Church in Turkey. It led to my captivated introduction to Turgay's indigenous worship songs. I offer my gratitude to Scott and Christine DeVries, Kaya Carvey, and Sema Yazgan for their guidance and help with lyric translations, and to my longtime friends (you know who you are) for their continued confidence and words of encouragement along the way.

I express my enduring thanks to my family. To Judd, Eric, and Billie, my three adult children, for their support of a crazy mom who went back to school late in life, and most especially to my husband, Jerry, for his loving patience and encouragement during this seven-year long process. His support was invaluable.

Soli DEO gloria!

Abbreviations

ASM	All Saints Moda
CD	*Christian Daily*
CCC [CRU]	Campus Crusade for Christ
CIA	Central Intelligence Agency
CT	*Christianity Today*
CTM	Classical Turkish music (makam music from the Ottoman Period—1299 through 1922)
DJ	*Digital Journal*
EJSP	*European Journal of Social Psychology*
FOREIGN AFF	*Foreign Affairs*
HASAT	Harvest Church Ministries
HIST RELIGIONS	*History of Religions*
IBMR	*International Bulletin of Missionary Research*
ILS PAPERS	*Institute of Liturgical Studies Papers*
IJFM	*International Journal of Frontier Missiology*
IPC	Istanbul Presbyterian Church
IRM	*International Review of Missions*
ITN	International Turkey Network
J RELIG	*Journal of Religion*

Abbreviations

MED ANTHROPOL Q	*Medical Anthropology Quarterly*
MESAB	*Middle East Studies Association Bulletin*
MF	*Mission Frontiers*
MINTS	Miami International Seminary
MIR	*Missiology: An International Review*
MBB	Muslim-Background Believer
Ottoman-Turkish Music	Classical Turkish Music (CTM) and Turkish Sanat Music (TSM)
PATTERNS PREJUDICE	*Patterns of Prejudice*
PW	*Publisher's Weekly*
QCA	Qualitative content analysis
TEK	Evangelical association of church leaders in Turkey
TFM	Turkish folk music
TPK	Turkish Protestant Church
TRT	Turkish Radio and Television Corporation
TSM	Turkish Sanat Music (Turkish art music in the Turkish language after 1923)
TW	Translated Western worship songs
WBC	*Word Biblical Commentary*
WEA	World Evangelical Alliance

Introduction

Music of the Heart

When I was born, like millions of other Turkish babies, the Hicaz makam[1] welcomed me. When a baby comes, a family elder chants a makam to the baby.[2] When mothers put them to sleep, they use the makam. At henna nights,[3] family members and friends sing makam songs. When I was circumcised at eight or nine years old, a family friend sang a little song. This is makam.

Can you separate Turkey from the makamlar?[4] I'm not talking about the six or seven million who live a modern lifestyle. I'm talking about seventy-four million Muslims, even nonbelievers who attend the *Bayram*[5] Festival Morning Prayer at the mosque, twice a year, where they sing the makam melody by the famous Ottoman composer, Itri. It's a hymn-type glorification. When you go for *Ramazan*[6] nights or if you watch Taraweeh [a long Islamic worship form] on TV during *Ramazan*, men and women sing a

---

1. The Hicaz makam is a particular Turkish melodic pattern.

2. The *shahada* (the Muslim profession of faith) is whispered in the ear, dedicating the child to Islam.

3. Henna night is a traditional all-female evening prior to a wedding during which the bride and her guests have their hands and feet temporarily tattooed.

4. Makam is singular. Makamlar and makam-s are plural.

5. *Bayram* is the Turkish word for a nationally celebrated holiday. This word is applicable to both secular and Muslim festivals.

6. *Ramazan* is the name for the thirty-day Islamic holy month, a time of fasting, prayer, and celebration.

1

special Arabic song in makam style together at the mosque. Millions of Muslims sing it. Makamlar are important.

I cannot separate the Alevi[7] families and Sunni[8] families much. Some are village people—some city people, so that some Sunnis in cities, some Alevis in villages, some Sunnis in villages, and some Alevis in cities sing it. It's everybody's song. It's there. As a culture, it's there. It is our melody. Seventy-four million Turkish people listen to it! The Greek Orthodox Church in Turkey uses makamlar! The Antakya Arab Church uses makamlar! If you go to the Assyrian Orthodox Church, they use makamlar! It is the music of the heart in Turkey![9]

PASTOR TURGAY ÜÇAL'S VIVID description reveals Turkey's indigenous people's deep connection to their music-culture. It also provides an inkling of the reason for selecting Turgay,[10] a well-respected local pastor of a Protestant church in Turkey, as the subject of my study. It was our second interview. I was sitting across from Turgay in his office, and he had just put his finger on the pulse of ethnodoxology—the "music of the heart."[11] It was at that moment that I, as an ethnodoxologist, recognized that Turgay's *emic* (insider) perspective had served as the impetus to create worship songs in an indigenous form.

In the past, translated choruses dominated the worship music of the All Saints Moda church (ASM) in Istanbul. Today, its musical expressions bridge the old and new, local and foreign. The worship, however, is outwardly defined or characterized by Turgay's Turkish makam songs.

The songs of this particular assembly came to my attention a few years after Turgay's music first emerged. Although regarded as controversial in many Turkish Protestant churches, his songs unite ASM's cultural heritage with Christian faith. The assembly was singing their faith in their traditional music system. This was a unique case, much like that of Roberta King with the Senufo of Côte d'Ivoire. As she aptly observed,

---

7. Alevi is the largest religious minority in Turkey.

8. Sunni is the largest branch of Islam in Turkey.

9. Üçal, interview, July 15, 2013.

10. Although Turgay has a brilliant mind and has realized many noteworthy achievements, he remains humble and approachable. In order to convey the reality of these character traits, I refer to him by his first name throughout this study.

11. Avery, "Music of the Heart," 13.

There was no need to try to convince people that they could use their own music to praise God. They were already doing it. There was no need to formulate anthropological arguments concerning form and function as it relates to music, no need to question whether secular musical forms and instruments could be employed in a Christian setting. It was already happening.[12]

Like King, I was delighted to see God at work through the people's music. Questions that come up in missiological circles and in churches where inculturation has not been introduced were being addressed in a real-life setting at ASM in Turkey. It provided a context in which to speak to issues on the inside of a people's worship practice instead of conjecturing from the *etic* (outsider) perspective.

Consequently, I decided to limit my study to the ASM community. I sensed that research among them would significantly contribute to the urban missiological and ethnodoxological literature and research in three ways:

1. It would provide data relative to the development and use of indigenous worship songs as tools for communication of the gospel. I would not need to question whether it could be done.

2. Since indigenous music was already happening in a local church in Turkey, it would be a unique study, making it possible to ask how and why cultural music makes a difference in the lives of believers.

3. It would serve as a critical case in testing a well-formed theory that inculturation of music has an important effect on identity and spiritual formation, by validating, contesting, or expanding that theory. Circumstances in the ASM assembly were already present for testing this theory.

But it was not just about the music. A combination of artistic expression and ASM's liturgy and theology was significantly affecting the maturing and vibrant body of Christ followers. A new tradition of Christian worship had taken shape. Consequently, during the middle stage of research, I adjusted my goals and enlarged my original topic of Turgay's songs into a broader ethnographical study of ASM's musico-liturgical inculturation of the worship event.

---

12. King, "Pathways in Christian Music Communication," 13.

The findings of Ruth Nicholls's study, "Catechisms and Chants: A Case for Using Liturgies in Ministry to Muslims" supports in theory what my research findings show in practice.[13] A Christian liturgy "informed and influenced by Islamic culture" fosters the development of spiritual growth within that worship event and serves the spiritual needs of Muslim seekers.

BACKGROUND

The Protestant Church in Turkey of approximately six to seven thousand worshipers is slowly growing, adding to around one hundred thousand Christians belonging to the existing ancient and Orthodox churches in Turkey.[14] Although this is encouraging, most Protestant churches in Turkey are fragile and ineffective. Sadly, credible reports claim that nine out of ten Muslims who come to faith leave the church within two years of making their decision.[15] Cross-cultural workers are searching for practical and effective ways to facilitate spiritual formation among Muslim seekers so that they might assist them on their journeys to spiritual maturity or Christlikeness.

We need a genuine passionate swell for ministry and mission through relevant worship practice. I argue in this study that the question of inculturation is non-negotiable, and for those who reach out to local people in an Islamic context, the answer is predicated on this premise.

RESEARCH DESIGN

This section summarizes the key parts of my research project. The following statements and questions provide the framework.

13. Nicholls, "Catechisms and Chants," ii.

14. In 1880, there were "6,000 members of the evangelical church in Turkey, meeting in over 100 congregations" (Wilson, "Striving Together for the Faith of the Gospel," 5). However, the one million massacred Armenians in the 1915 genocide during the First World War and the exodus during the Turkish War of Independence that followed (1919–1923) effectively blotted out one hundred years of missionary work and any fruit of this labor. It wasn't until the 1960s that evangelism began again. See chapter 1 for more on the history of the Protestant church in Turkey.

15. Keating, "State of the Turkish Church," 3. [Ryan Keating was a long-term worker in Turkey, that from 2012 to 2016 periodically sent out a report on the state of the church via news4marmara, an online closed source of information for workers. He was banned from entering Turkey in 2017, and now ministers in Cyprus.]

Purpose and Goal

The chief purpose of this research is twofold: (1) to identify the stimuli in the life of Turgay Üçal that prompted the inception of musico-liturgical inculturation, and (2) to explore the impact of his indigenous worship songs on the lives of the ASM assembly members in Istanbul, Turkey.

Significance

Christianity in Turkey is still identified as a Western religion, and the people in Turkey have not responded in word and song to the universal call of Jesus. There is a gap between inculturation theory and practice. Given the predominantly Westernized churches in Turkey, music—with its communicational properties and proven effectiveness in advancing the *missio Dei*—is one area where inculturation needs to take place.

Turkish makam songs[16] in the ASM assembly echo that theme and present new comparative possibilities in the process. The inculturation of worship at the church represents a model of worship practice that strikes a balance between indigenous values and syncretism.[17] As a result of fostering Christian identity and spiritual formation, believers have become fully local and authentically followers of Christ.

Through this work, I intend to enrich the scope of the conversation and practice of ethnodoxology, providing relevant data on the development of how mission work can be done globally through an investigation of the use of indigenous hymnody and its contributions to the inculturation of worship. I am hopeful that the results of this investigation will encourage other church leaders within Turkey to consider the appropriateness of inculturation and use of local music in worship, ministry, and witness, while remaining in line with the global Protestant hermeneutical community. It may also offer valuable insights and practical solutions for the many different people groups in the world who struggle with how the good news relates to cultural music in their particular contexts.

Central Research Issue

The aim of this research is to discover what prompted Turgay Üçal to inculturate the worship practice of the ASM faith assembly and to explore the effects of his indigenous hymns on the congregants.

16. *Sanat* (or art) music style.
17. Stetzer, "Avoiding the Pitfall of Syncretism," lines 22–24.

Introduction: Music of the Heart

Research Questions

1. What significant events and influences in Turgay's life led to the inception of musico-liturgical inculturation?

2. What are the key themes in Turgay's eighty-song anthology of indigenous songs?

3. What is the role of music in the worship practice of ASM?

4. How do Turgay's songs affectively, cognitively, and behaviorally impact the everyday lives of ASM congregants?

Definition of Terms

For the purposes of this study, I define the following terms:

1. *Culturally appropriate worship*: The *rightness* of a worship practice in a local setting—including theology and aesthetic ideals—related to a specific understanding of how God reveals himself in worship.

2. *Ethnodoxology*: "The study of the worship of God in the world's cultures; the theological and practical study of how and why people of other cultures praise and glorify the true and living God."[18]

3. *Ethnomusicology*: "The study of music in the context of human life."[19]

4. *Form and function*: Two major alternate evangelical views deal with form and meaning, or message. While Charles Kraft separates form from meaning,[20] Paul Hiebert teaches that meaning exists in the correspondence between reality and Reality, claiming that there is an external Reality to which meanings refer.[21] Forms can be—but are not by definition—neutral. In agreement with Kraft, Turgay stated, "Everything can be used to God's glory. Objects can be redefined."[22]

5. *Inculturation*: A comprehensive term expressing the relationship between the gospel and culture. It refers to the dynamic translation of the gospel into the culture of local churches. The process of inculturation

---

18. Shubin, "Worship that Moves the Soul," 10–15.
19. Titon, *Worlds of Music*, xiii.
20. Kraft, *Christianity in Culture*, loc. 1927.
21. Hiebert, "Form and Meaning in Contextualization," 104.
22. Üçal, interview, February 9, 2015.

is "an intuitive process of finding one's faith and religious identity in the context of one's cultural world."[23]

6. *Indigenous hymnody*: Worship songs that reflect the language, local music system, and song forms of a particular society.

7. *Music-culture*: For this study, I use Jeff Todd Titon's definition of music-culture: "A group's total involvement with music: ideas, actions, institutions, material objects—everything that has to do with music."[24]

8. *Musico-liturgical*: A term referring to the musical and ceremonial elements of Christian worship.

9. *Orality*: Malcolm Hartnell describes orality as "the condition or quality of a society that either has minimal knowledge of writing or prefers not to employ writing as the primary means for acquiring or exchanging information."[25]

10. *Identity*: Characteristics of people or groups that make them different from others. The identity of a believer is in Christ, through a spiritual relationship in need of ongoing transformation.

11. *Spiritual formation*: The process of becoming more like Christ through the power of the Holy Spirit and the guidance of his Word. This includes specific practices such as prayer, the study of Scripture, worship, silence, and service, as modeled after the practices and behaviors of Christ and the early church.

Delimitations

1. I delimited the research to a local church community in Istanbul, Turkey, All Saints Moda and its pastor/music maker, Turgay Üçal. It is a study of musico-liturgical inculturation, with a focus that permits deeper study into the worship event and its impact on congregants. This is an embedded case study.

2. I delimited the music in this research to eighty songs Turgay had created by the time I began studying his song texts in 2013. The ASM 2013–2015 prayer books provided the song texts, and I transcribed approximately thirty-five of the melodies from digital recordings I

23. Magesa, *Anatomy of Culture*, loc. 3303.
24. Titon, *Worlds of Music*, 4.
25. Hartnell, "Oral Contextualization," 9–10.

made during Sunday services.[26] I selected Turgay's corpus of worship songs as a focal point in this study, because it was an emerging indigenous music style that was gaining acceptance outside his local church and Turkey.

3. I delimited this research to the English language. Though the liturgical worship practice prayer books were written in the Turkish mother tongue, I accessed them through English-translated printed copies. Interviews with the primary subject, Turgay, and six of the eighteen research respondents were conducted in English. When respondents spoke only Turkish, interviews were conducted with the aid of translators.

Assumptions

1. I assume that the need for a sense of belonging in worship is universal.

2. I assume that local song and inculturated worship as practiced at ASM are a means through which national peoples can feel at home and attain a sense of belonging.

3. I assume that Turgay's inculturation of musico-liturgical worship at ASM effectively fosters the development of identity and spiritual formation as measured through qualitative research.

4. I assume that local song and inculturated worship practice is essential for the healthy long life of a church's ministry and witness.

OVERVIEW

This qualitative applied case study focuses on a single church—ASM in Istanbul, Turkey—and its pastor—Turgay Üçal. Exploring historical and socioreligious influences that motivated Turgay to initiate musico-liturgical inculturation of ASM's worship practice, this research details the role of his hymnody in the worship event and its impact on believers' identities and spiritual formation, within the scope of King's matrix of global church music.[27]

---

26. The other forty-five songs were previously transcribed.
27. King, "Beginnings," 13.

In this introduction, I provided the background and significance of the study, its purpose, central research issue, and research questions. I present the remainder of the study in three parts.

In part 1, comprised of chapters 1–3, I situate the investigation in its sociohistorical and music-cultural contexts, presenting the study's contribution to the literature, my theoretical framework, my rationale for the research design of applied case study, and the methodologies employed.

In part 2, comprised of chapters 4–6, I present the findings and data analysis revealing the significance of Turgay's indigenous songs and their impact on the life of ASM's assembly. In chapter 4, I examine Turgay's life story, highlighting his journey to faith and various leadership roles that led to his music making and inculturation of ASM's worship event. In chapter 5, I examine the role of music in the church's liturgical practice in addition to applying the mapping of the ritual. In chapter 6, I authenticate a positive correlation between Turgay's songs and the strengthened self-identities and spiritual formation of ASM assembly members.

Part 3 is comprised of the final two chapters of this study. In chapter 7, I describe the repertoire and aesthetics of the assembly's preferred music system (Turkey's traditional art music system), applying Titon's six intertwined elements of music. This is followed by the final chapter, in which I summarize the study and chart a way forward in light of my findings. The research findings show that ASM's musico-liturgical inculturation of worship is a viable model for a local church in a Muslim culture with the vision to provide culturally appropriate songs and other worship forms. Those who participate in inculturated worship are inclined to grow in their development of Christian identity and spiritual formation, leading to their equipping and empowerment for witness. Finally, I recommend areas for further research.

Exploring Turkey's East-West Musical Milieu

We Turks,

Are we Asians,

or Europeans?

Are we Eastern,

or Anatolian,

or Western?

Who are we?

—Bozkurt Güvenç[1]

---

1. Güvenç, "We Turks," lines 1–3 and 23–26.

1

Music Making in Turkey and Missionary Endeavors

The usually crowded streets of Istanbul are empty on Sunday morning as we walk to ASM for the 11 a.m. worship service. Everyone else is most likely asleep. In Turkey, one of the notable differences from the US or Europe is the culture of religion. Five times a day, the *ezan*[1] calls Muslims to prayer. These melodies are impossible to ignore. Near the end of Pastor Turgay's sermon, the electronically amplified voice of the *muezzin*[2] rings out from the mosque behind the church. The traditional Turkish musical system used to recite the Muslim call to prayer is the same as the ASM assembly's call to worship, reinforcing Turgay's commitment to inculturation.[3]

IN THIS CHAPTER, I focus on the context of the study, including Turkey's music-culture and Martin Stokes's four dimensions that define it: (1) music and politics (2) music and migration (3) music and globalization, and (4) music and belief systems.[4] This music-culture is the incubator for Turgay Üçal's hymnody. Music is an ideal avenue for exploring Turkey's religious and sociocultural history and traditions as they relate to the background of this urban church research.

1. Call to prayer.
2. The man who calls Muslims to prayer from the minaret of a mosque.
3. Whittaker, field notes, 2013–2015.
4. Stokes, "Music," 96–106.

13

Part One: Exploring Turkey's East-West Musical Milieu

BACKGROUND

Remnants of the six-hundred-year Ottoman Empire that once contained people of many different cultures, languages, and religions still exist within present-day Turkey. Consequently, the peoples of Turkey have a multicultural, multiethnic history.[5] Its geographical location as a crossroad of world trade routes between Europe, the Middle East, and Africa as well as Central Asia and the Caucasus enhances Turkey's diversity. Uniquely positioned as a transcontinental country in Eurasia (95 percent of Turkey lies in Asia and five percent in Europe), Turkey is bordered by eight countries and is simultaneously encircled by seas on three sides (see map 1).

Map 1: Map of Turkey

Turkey is characterized not only by its geographical location but also by its largest and most cosmopolitan city, Istanbul. The 2017 official population estimate of Istanbul was fourteen million.[6] A more realistic—but un-official—population estimate places the number at twenty million.[7] Known as the country's economic and cultural center, Istanbul stands alongside London, Paris, and Moscow as one of the four anchor megacities of Europe.[8]

5. For a singular and insightful account of the country's history, see Zürcher's *Turkey: A Modern History*. For a comprehensive look at how the modern Middle East (including Turkey) emerged after the First World War, see *A Peace to End All Peace* by Fromkin.

6. City Population, "Istanbul," website.

7. Bates, *Music in Turkey*, xxiv.

8. Jones Lange LaSalle, "Istanbul Among Top Four Megacities of Europe," title.

Currently, Istanbul plays an eminent role in bridging East and West music cultures, similar to the way in which this great metropolis stretches across two continents, divided and defined by the Bosporus waterway (see map 2).

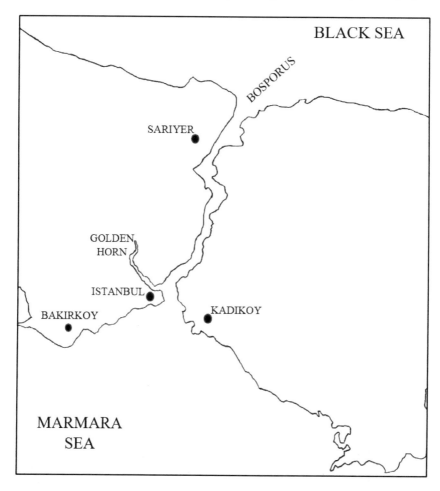

Map 2: Map of Istanbul

Turkey's musical influences range from the music of the Greeks, Arabs, Persians, Armenians, and Balkans to the eleventh-century elements of both Türkic and pre-Türkic influences of Central Asia to the Ottoman music, the Sufi influence, and above all, the Byzantine culture.[9] Turkish music historians, however, usually disregard the influence of the non-Islamic

9. Stokes, "Republic of Turkey," 168–79.

cultures. Even so, the themes of national and regional identity related to present-day music in Turkey are noteworthy. In the following section, I analyze these unique musical understandings and practices, but first, what is a music-culture?

MUSIC-CULTURE

Music-culture is a term that neatly summarizes all the factors in a music event that blend to make sense within a cultural context. It adds to the understanding of a culture and is a group's total engagement with music—it is everything that contributes to how music functions in meaningful ways for both personal and group expression. According to Jeff Todd Titon, the four components of music-culture are (1) a community's ideas about music; (2) activities involving music; (3) repertoires of music, comprising style, genres, texts, composition, transmission, and movement; and (4) the material features of music—the tangible objects, primarily musical instruments, songbooks, sheet music, CDs, music videos, TV, and the computer.[10]

Music in Turkey today is generally understood in four broad classifications: *Klasik Türk müziği* (classical or religious Turkish music, 1299–1922), featuring lyrics that are extensively borrowed from Arabic and Persian;[11] *Türk Sanat Müziği* (art music in the Turkish language after 1923);[12] *Türk halk müziği* or *türkü* (Turkish folk music);[13] and Türk *pop müziği* (Turkish popular music).[14] Classical Turkish classical music was favored in urban areas, the Sultan's palaces, and the Sufi houses of worship (*tekkes*), while *sanat* music—a derivative of classical music—refers to contemporary art songs in the modern Turkish language.[15] [Turkish *sanat*, or art music is the preferred music style of Turgay and the ASM church community]. *Halk* music (folk) is viewed as the music of the Anatolian countryside and peasantry. Finally, popular music—a more diverse collection—includes hybrids of Balkan or Middle Eastern music, such as arabesque, in addition to Turkish-language global pop. Alongside American pop music, a wider spectrum of music genres is available through globalized media. To

10. Titon, *World of Music*, 19–31.

11. Feldman, "Ottoman Music," 1–11.

12. Reinhard and Stokes, "Turkey IV: Art Music," 9–19.

13. Stokes, "Turkey II: Folk Music," 2–8.

14. Reinhard and Stokes, "Turkey V: Popular Music," 19–22.

15. Bates, *Music in Turkey*, 29.

be sure, a music-culture first reflects its own culture with all its historical, political, economic, and aesthetic influences.

CONTEXT

In the following sections, I examine Turkey's music-cultures within the context of the country's major social transformations since the earliest decades of the New Republic: politics, migration, and globalization. I also look at Turkey's major belief system and the missionary influence on the Protestant Church in Turkey.

Music and Politics

Political events in Turkey have had a significant impact on its music, especially in the twentieth century. Turkey's geographical location and a six-century-long societal history encompass Arab, Balkan, and Asian peoples, effectively bringing different people face-to-face in political and historical events through clashes and conquests. The establishment of the Turkish Republic in 1923 led to great change for the newly birthed nation, with its diverse music coming under particular scrutiny. The social engineering efforts of the revolutionary founder of the Republic of Turkey, Mustafa Kemal Atatürk, triggered a new national music he thought original and that helped form and support a unified Turkish identity.[16] Atatürk's goal was to break with the past and feature the modern in the new nation-state, replacing the Ottoman Empire's political Islam with separation of state and religion; thus he and his reformers looked to the West, minimizing the impact of neighboring Islamic nations on its new secular-state ideology.

Soon afterward, Western arrangements of Turkish folk music became the new national music—Eastern melodies with Western harmony[17]—while

---

16. In contrast, the Ottoman Empire was diverse, both religiously and ethnically. The motto "How happy is the one who says, 'I am a Turk'" was first used in a speech by Atatürk in 1933. In 1972, the Ministry of National Education of the Republic of Turkey added this motto to the primary school student oath. (The motto was removed from the oath in 2013).

17. "The systematic elevation of rural folk music was initiated with archival collection" (Reinhard and Stokes, "Turkey II, Folk Music"). Following the establishment of the Republic of Turkey, Atatürk decreed the collecting of Turkish-language folk songs from across Anatolia, resulting in tens of thousands of songs being recorded. Western-trained musicians applied harmonization to the simple rural songs, and mass choruses and orchestras of indigenous folk instruments performed them on public Turkish radio and television (TRT) broadcasts. This genre of musical expression formed the foundation of

the reformers eschewed Ottoman classical music as a relic—an outdated inheritance of an imperial civilization. But the music reformers of Atatürk's era failed to stamp out the Eastern music. It made a comeback after a few years. The period of music reformism is no more; however, there remains a vibrant quest for national cultural modernization.

Fiske emphasizes the need for multiple social allegiances today.[18] His perspective, in part, is reflected in the growing musical contribution of villagers who migrate to the cities of Turkey.

Music and Migration

Istanbul's rich and exciting music culture has been affected by a long-established tradition of assimilation of immigrants from many regions, including rural Anatolia. Urban art music and folk music as well as the more recent musics and musical instruments are brought mostly through chain immigration.[19] "In large and provincial cities, *dernek* or *cemiyet* [folk music clubs] teach the reformulated folk music style to newly arrived rural migrants as well as young urbanites."[20]

Generally speaking, the folk styles are similar across all Turkish regions. Many folk songs are traditional and are sung nationally. Consequently, one must not approach contemporary Turkish folk music as though it exists in isolated pockets of the countryside. It is the product of movement between village and city, and as musician Orhan Gencebay notes, "Istanbul is a place where villages come together."[21] In other words, the thriving metropolis of Istanbul is a collection of villages where different nationalities and cultures meet. But Istanbul is more than a place where national music traditions have historically combined; it is also a place where one can experience the musics of globalization.

---

a government-controlled music repertoire called *türkü*, which means "Turkish-language ballad." Songs drawn from various language/ethnic groups (Armenian, Kurdish, Laz, Zazaki, and others) were adapted or translated into Turkish on the spot or later in Ankara. A *türkü* song must be sung in Turkish and not associated with religious activities or meanings. The authorship of most folk music is unknown.

18. Fiske, *Understanding Popular Culture*, 24.

19. *Chain immigration* is the social process whereby immigrants from a particular town are followed by other family members and friends who settle in the same neighborhoods in new (usually urban) locations in the home country.

20. Stokes, "Turkey II: Folk Music," 2–8.

21. Gencebay quote in Akkaya and Fehmiye, *60'lardan*, 246.

Music and Globalization

> Globalization does not signal the erasure of local difference, but
> in a strange way its converse; it revalidates and reconstitutes place,
> locality and difference.[22]

Amid Europeanization, some believe that "Istanbul is reacting like a micro-
cosm of globalization: Every move upward, outward, westward, and forward
is met with resistance and even backlash."[23] As a megacity, the postmodern
cultural world of Istanbul knows tension, fragmentation, and subcultural
differences. In "Istanbulites and Others: The Cultural Cosmology of Being
Middle Class in the Era of Globalism," Ayşe Öncü claims, "A plurality of
social groups and cultures coexist . . . often separated from one another
as the hard-edged pieces of a mosaic."[24] These shifting fragments of social
identities remain divided along secular, religious, sectarian, and ethnic lines:
the rich and the poor, Sunni and Alevi, Christian and Jew minorities, the
Turk, Kurd, Arab, and Roma, among others. The problems posed by such an
assemblage are considerable. They are reminiscent of Samuel Huntington's
article "The Clash of Civilizations"[25] in which he claimed that the next global
disruptions would be along the fault lines of cultural and religious identities and that Turkey was one of those designated as a torn country—torn
between its secular Westernism and an Islamic revival.

Against the backdrop of Huntington's case, the growing coexistence
of Eastern and Western elements in Turkish music can be considered an
indication of how the people of Turkey see themselves as having both an
Eastern and a Western identity. Elaborating on this statement in "Orchestrating Multiple Eastern-Western Identities through Music: A Turkish
Story," Itri observes that although Turkey may be struggling politically
with its Western outlook and Eastern origins, people seem to be culturally
more at ease with themselves and their dual Eastern-Western characteristics, chiefly in popular music.[26] The author argues that we can and do have
multiple identities and that music is an ideal platform where those identities are both experienced and expressed. We could express this duality
with the word *bi-musicality*, a term coined by ethnomusicologist Mantle

22. Watts, "Mapping Meaning, Denoting Difference," 10.
23. Frommers, "Istanbul," lines 15–17.
24. Öncü, "Istanbulites and Others," 95.
25. Huntington, "Clash of Civilizations," 42.
26. Toksöz, "Orchestrating Multiple Eastern-Western Identities," 83.

Hood[27] and applied to music in the same way a linguist refers to someone who speaks two languages.

Koray Değirmenci expands our concept of musical identities even further in a vivid description of how various modes of Western European, American, and Middle Eastern popular genres are mediated to the general audience in Turkey:

> Music markets toss myriad sounds into the air, blending them so as to render them indistinguishable from one another. A clarinet *taksim* (improvisation) gives way to a piece that begins with a woman's voice heavily processed with a synthesizer and accompanied by a *ney* improvisation. This is followed by the rapping of the famous Turkish hip-hop artist, Ceza, during which Sufi philosophy is praised. An *oyun havas* (dance tune) signature to Roma (gypsy) weddings in Turkey gradually envelops these sounds along Istiklal Avenue, located in the most vibrant district of Istanbul, Pera.[28]

Places of juxtaposition such as these are considered *global spaces*— places where the local and the global coexist. Today's music in Turkey is eclectic. There are various genres such as folk and art music, pop music, opera, and Western classical music, Anatolian rock, rap, hip-hop, jazz, heavy metal, *fasil*,[29] *arabesk*,[30] new age, world music, Egyptian popular music translated to Turkish, belly dancing (borrowed from Eastern associations), and so on. Aytar, Volkan, and Keskin report that Istanbul welcomes diverse kinds of music and borrows musical types from different social and cultural groups.[31]

Stokes speaks to the same point when he claims that hybrid genres are authentic, organically connected to the social life and cultural aspirations of particular localities.[32] One can aptly conclude that since Eastern and Western characteristics can coexist in the same musical piece, they can also coexist in the identity of the listeners.

We attribute this situation to the effects of migration and information technology (IT), a driving factor in the process of globalization. IT has been the catalyst for global integration. As Toksöz writes, "Multiple

27. Hood, "Challenge of 'Bi-Musicality,'" 55–59.
28. Değirmenci, *Creating Global Music in Turkey*, 1.
29. See glossary for definition.
30. See glossary for definition.
31. Aytar et al., "Construction of Spaces of Music in Istanbul," 150.
32. Stokes, "Republic of Turkey," 60.

identities are more common in places where globalization has made the biggest impact, as well as the places where identities have been historically complex."[33] She adds, "Music's role in this is potentially powerful, as shown in the case of Turkey."[34] On that consideration, I turn my attention to the context of music and the belief system.

Music and Belief System

According to Jenny White, it is clear from many surveys on identity that being Turkish and being Muslim are primary.[35] The Islamic majority population in Turkey is Sunni, with some estimates suggesting that 20 to 40 percent of Turkey's population today is Alevi-Bektashi. Alevism is alternately described as "a heterodox offshoot of Iran's Shi'ites,"[36] or according to the General Chairman of the United Federation of Alevi-Bektasi Organizations, "a unique philosophy, a faith, a way of life . . . peculiar to Anatolia."[37] The remainder is either secular Muslim or engaged in a large unknown number of *tarikats*[38] (religious brotherhoods), mostly with a Sufi orientation.[39]

Turkey is a country with shared historical and common roots, both ceremonially and musically, among the three Abrahamic religions. As a result of the Ottoman conquest of Constantinople in 1453, Istanbul became the cultural epicenter of the Orient, where Christians, Jews, and Muslims were subjects and servants of the Ottoman ruler.

> Musicians and poets, whether they were Persian, Arab, Greek, Armenian, Indian or Jewish, were all equally welcome at the Sultan's court. The outcome was a magical melodic amalgam, meaning Sephardic Jews combined their ritual Hebrew texts with Sufi songs, or when Christian composers and musicians like Zaharay taught Ottoman music in the harem.[40]

It was a golden age of symbiosis of widely differing cultures. But from 1950 forward, reactions to Atatürk's ideas and principles "often took the

---

33. Toksöz, "Orchestrating Multiple Eastern-Western Identities through Music," 85.
34. Toksöz, "Orchestrating Multiple Eastern-Western Identities through Music," 96.
35. White, *Muslim Nationalism and the New Turks*, 21.
36. Stocks, "Music," 101.
37. Dogan, "Turkey: The Alevi Faith," lines 14–16.
38. See glossary for definition.
39. Ozturk, *Eye of the Heart*, 92–101.
40. Yeşilçay, "One God, Psalms and Hymns," 42.

form of economic liberalism linked to religious conservatism."[41] Stokes sees a similar situation in musical culture, in terms of the Islamic singing tradition that survived—Qur'an and Mevlid recitation, the call to prayer, and hymn (ilahi)—because "they were embedded unobtrusively in the everyday devotional practices and soundscapes of the Muslim majority."[42]

Nevertheless, the phrase "Islamic religious music" is a misnomer to Sunni Muslims. Similar to those Protestant denominations influenced by theologian John Calvin as well as to the more conservative branches of Judaism, those who practice Orthodox Islam in Turkey are troubled about music's power to stimulate the lower passions (nafs). As a result, musical expressions that combine pitch and rhythm (normally classified as music in Western culture) are distinguished by a higher-level category called non-musiqa (non-music) and a lower-level category called musiqa (music). All genres of non-musiqa—including the call to prayer, recitation of the Qur'an, and chanted religious poetry—are considered halal (lawful or permissible). Musical recitation (qur'anic cantillation) represents the religion's oral approach to religious texts, and since the inception of Islam, this vocal style has been regarded as 'reading' instead of 'singing,' meaning these verbal sounds are culturally and religiously defined as non-music.

Devotional music is quite varied, ranging from folk music to Mevlevi and Alevi Sufi music. It includes a vocal form, ilahi (hymn or a sung prayer). It also includes particular instrumental pieces and songs of a mystical nature sung by both Alevi aşık folk poets[43] and the ummah, lay members of the Sunni community. According to Saktanber,[44] the private radio stations geared toward the general Islamic population in general or to youth in particular tend to play largely folk ballads (türkü). She reasons that the Islamic youth tend to listen to folk music as a consequence of their search for a fixed authentic identity, with the desire of being "first and foremost a dedicated Muslim . . . throughout several social allegiances."[45]

But, then again, since the early 1990s, a new popular religious subculture has grown. In truth, this youth subculture has created a strong sense

41. Stokes, "Music," 101.

42. Stokes, "Music," 3.

43. Aşık poetry refers to poetry about the love of God. The term literally means "the one in love with God" in Turkish.

44. Saktanber, "We Pray Like You Have Fun," 265.

45. Saktanber, "We Pray Like You Have Fun," 267.

of national identity that has always had a strongly religious nuance.[46] This subculture combines rock music with an Islamic message and calls it *yesil,* or "green" pop, in a subtle reference to Islam's traditional color. [47] Stokes describes this genre as similar to the secular *arabesk* song form in vocal techniques and musical and lyrical language.

A typical Sunni Muslim embraces Sufism. Steven Schwartz claims that most Muslims in Turkey "are Sufi either by identification with the normative Sunnism . . . or by participation in Sufi orders as well as widespread, part-time study circles and other voluntary communities that teach an esoteric Islam."[48] Thus, both classical music and folk music play an important role in their lives; in the case of the Mevlevi Sufi Order, it is both classical and folk, whereas, in the Alevi Sufi tradition, it is simply folk.

While there are similarities between practices of the famous Mevlevi Order of the Whirling Dervishes and those of the Alevis, they are not the same. In contrast to the Mevlevis, Alevis concentrate on spiritual activities in *cems* (worship ceremonies) that include the essential of the *semah* (ceremonial dance) accompanied by the *bağlama* (a long-necked, fat-bodied guitar-like instrument) and mystical poetry sung in Turkish.[49] These events also "serve to reinforce social solidarity and correctness of behavior . . .,"[50] as Irene Markoff states. The Alevis are closely related to the Bektasi Sufi brotherhood in Turkey, named after Hajji Bektash Walli (1209–1271) of Anatolia.

In my discussion of four different music contexts in Turkey (politics, migration, globalization, and the belief system), I draw upon continuing research work. While rooted in popular experience, the research is situated in Turkey's major cities, where music provides a means of "placing oneself

46. Stokes, *Republic of Love*, 22.

47. Stokes, *Republic of Love*, 22. "There are other forms of *yesil* pop, such as *yeni ilahi* (new hymn for God), *zikr* pop, and so forth. In them, secular-sounding string choruses and *darbuka*-s of *arabesk* are usually replaced by the *ney* and the *def* instruments with spiritual overtones."

48. Schwartz, "How Many Sufis are there in Islam?," lines 75–78.

49. A *cemevi* is known as a worship house (a house of gathering) for Alevis in Turkey. The Alevis believe in the unity of Allah, Muhammad, and Ali, but Muhammad and Ali represent Allah's light rather than God himself. They follow the "Twelver theology." The latter refers to the belief that the community's leadership after Muhammad was authorized as Muhammad's daughter Fatima, Ali, and his eleven subsequent successors that together comprise the Fourteen Infallible and are considered far above the other major prophets in righteousness and divine knowledge.

50. Markoff, "Introduction to Sufi Music and Ritual in Turkey," 159.

in relation to others."[51] Nowhere is that contrast more obvious than the music that has been brought and taught by the latest wave of foreign missions, starting in the 1960s, and still continuing today.

IMPACT OF FOREIGN MISSIONS ON LOCAL WORSHIP PRACTICE

> "The church divided our family relations. They say, 'Oh, I hate that music. It reminds me of Islam.'"[52]

Anatolia—often called the "cradle of civilization"—can also be called the cradle of Christianity, as it was in Antioch that disciples were first called Christians,[53] and the minority peoples of eastern Anatolia were among the first non-Jews to accept the new religion. But while Asia Minor and Anatolia's early Christian history is well documented, the Christian population of Turkey is rapidly disappearing. Over the past century, Turkey's Christian population has experienced a reduction from 20 percent to less than 0.01 percent. This drop in population is largely a result of the Armenian Genocide (1915), Greek Genocide (1914–1923), and the ensuing population exchanges of Turkey's Christians with Greece's Muslims and the forced mass departure of Armenians, Assyrians, Greeks, and Georgians after the collapse of the Ottoman Empire. These atrocities resulted in an almost entirely Muslim-Turkish country. Some consider Christianity in Turkey today an endangered species,[54] and others believe that churches are on the verge of extinction.[55] Nonetheless, hopeful regional Christian leaders believe that the key to regional stability is to recognize a Christian presence and to allow the displaced believers to return and prosper.[56]

While there have been religious conflicts among the three Abrahamic faiths in Turkey, there has also been rich cultural interchange over centuries that continues into the twenty-first century. For many, the Ottoman Empire serves as a symbol of Muslim-Christian-Jewish encounters. As early as 1921, new forms of inculturation were explored. Missionaries began researching the host culture for the positive things they could add to

---

51. Keyder, *Istanbul: Between the Global and the Local*, 121.

52. Üçal, interview, July 15, 2013.

53. Acts 11:26.

54. Chastain, "Endangered Species," lines 1–4.

55. Bulut, "Churches in Turkey on the Verge of Extinction," lines 1–6.

56. Caballero, "Christian Presence Key to Mideast stability," lines 1–3.

their life, realizing how much contact with the culture would enhance their lives.[57] In this way, the national culture came to be appreciated.

But what about today? Have we seen the importance of taking that next step, a cultural exchange in Christian worship as we draw near to the end of the twenty-first century? The process of inculturation is "an intuitive process of finding one's faith and religious identity in the context of one's cultural world," according to Magesa.[58] Sadly, earlier experiments in inculturation did not remain in favor for long. Most subsequent approaches to evangelization and church planting in Turkey have bypassed local culture, in favor of westernizing the church.

Istanbulites speak a number of languages, but the Islamic government officially acknowledges only a few religious traditions: Islam, Christianity, and Judaism. Islam is the principal religion in Turkey, with 99.9 percent of the inhabitants Muslim, followed by Christianity and Judaism with a combined percentage of 0.1.[59] Most churches in the country are largely remnants of the Armenian, Nestorian, Jacobite Syrian and Eastern Orthodox traditions.

Since the emergence of Protestant churches around thirty-five years ago, they have been required to register with the state as foundations, instead of religious organizations, and clergy are forbidden from training in-country. Foreign Christians make up 60 percent of church leaders, while national Christian leaders amount to approximately 40 percent and are supported by a variety of Western church denominations. However, churches in Turkey avoid denominational labels in order to keep from confusing Muslim seekers. The congregations self-identify as Protestants, because there is no Turkish word for *evangelical*. Church members include Muslim background believers (MBBs), as well as converts from Armenian and Orthodox traditions, atheists and the unaffiliated.

In Table 1, "Abrahamic Faiths in Turkey," I specify the number of followers for the country's major faiths as listed in the *CIA World Factbook*

---

57. Walter, "Missionary Qualifications," 545–53.

58. Magesa, *Anatomy of Inculturation*, loc. 3303.

59. CIA, "Turkey," website. There is conflicting data on this topic. Though the CIA and the Turkish government claim that more than 99 percent of the population is Muslim, independent polling organizations give different results. For example, WorldAtlas claims that Sunni Islam comprises only 65 percent, followed by 13 percent unaffiliated Islam (78 percent of the total population), the irreligious, Christianity, and all other faiths.

2016, and I apply Bevans and Schroeder's three-type theology.[60] (Judaism and Islam are not included in their coverage).

Table 1: The Abrahamic Faiths in Turkey

FAITHS	Arrival in Turkey	Followers		Theology Type	Worship Format	Musical Development
JUDAISM		less than 0.02%				
-Jews	4th C BC		17,000		Ritual	Indigenization
CHRISTIANITY		less than 0.1%				
CATHOLIC	1st C		35,000	A/C	Ritual	Indigenization
-Byzantine -Chaldean -Latin -Armenian						
EASTERN ORTHODOX			8,000	A/C	Ritual	Indigenization
-Greek -Syriac	1st C					
ORIENTAL ORTHODOX			50,000	A/C	Ritual	Indigenization
-Armenian (Apostolic)	1st C					
PROTESTANT						
-ASM	1996		100	A/C	*Liturgical*	*Importation* *Adaptation* *Alteration* *Indigenization* *Internationalizatio*
-Armenian -Other evangelicals	1846 1970s		400 5,000-6,000	A/C	*Mostly Non-liturgical*	*Importation* *Adaptation* *Alternation* *Imitation*
ISLAM		99.9%				
-Sunni	11th C		63-65 million		Ritual	Indigenization
-Alevi	11th C		13-15 million		Ritual	Indigenization

KEY: A = Mission as Saving Souls and Extending the Church, C=Mission as Commitment to Liberation and Transformation, A/C = both theologies.

I also identify the Christian worship formats in terms of ritual (liturgical) and non-ritual (non-liturgical). Non-liturgical evangelical Protestants refer to their meeting as a worship service. The order of service is typically a three-part form: an extended time of singing, a sermon, and an invitation to accept Christ. In contrast, liturgical evangelical Protestants are those who advocate for weekly Eucharist and recognition of the church year and make use of ritual, gesture, bodily action, vestments, and other rites.

In the sixth column of this table, I draw from James Krabill's "six stages of music development: importation, adaptation, alteration, imitation,

60. Bevans and Schroeder, *Constants in Context*, 32.

indigenization, and internationalization," for an adaptation that illustrates the current stages within Turkey's different faiths.[61] His disclaimer: while these stages are typical, a linear progression is not a given. The musical changes may or may not follow this order or move through every stage.

In the *importation* stage, all hymn tunes, texts, and rhythms originate with foreigners and are introduced by the Western missionary. These imported songs are then locally translated, and Turkified in one way or another in the *adaptation* stage, making them more suitable and understandable for worshipers in the new locale.

Moving deeper into the process, the *alteration* stage involves replacing or otherwise significantly modifying some part of the foreign hymn (tune, text, or rhythm) with an indigenous form. Locally composed worship music (tunes, texts, and rhythms) replicates a Western genre in the *imitation* stage. The *indigenization* stage is where tunes, texts, and rhythms are locally produced in local musical forms and styles. Lastly, in the *internationalization* stage, the worship hymns and choruses (tunes, texts, and rhythms) from both the global church and the local context become integrated into the life and worship of the church. It makes clear that ASM, unlike other Protestant churches in Turkey, bypassed the imitation phase and progressed to the last two stages of music development: indigenization and internationalization.

Turkey's Protestant evangelical community is young and tiny in comparison to the Muslim-majority population, and its mission history has a non-inculturated gospel message glaringly obvious in the worship practice of today. Yet, All Saints Moda—one of the four largest churches in Istanbul—is criticized as being syncretistic, while holding to a unique Istanbuli-influenced music and liturgy that gives evidence of the efficacy of inculturation.

SUMMARY

Despite prevailing circumstances of politics, migration, globalization, religion, or mission history, the people of God worship in song, and it is out of this reality that my research proceeded. I sought to learn how musico-liturgical inculturation was influencing Istanbuli Christian identity and spiritual formation within the ASM church community, and specifically, how the body of believers matured through worship songs. Taking into account the cultural and religious context in which ASM is situated, I next present the missiological and theoretical framework that guided this research.

---

61. Krabill, "Encounters," 70–75.

2

Trodden Mission Paths

A public confession of Christ as Savior is a significant event in the life of a new believer in Turkey.

For weeks Bilge has looked forward to this momentous occasion.
After Bilge is baptized at the back of the sanctuary,[1] Pastor Turgay begins a slow, short chant invoking God's mercy.

O Lord, help us

O Lord, have mercy

Lord, have mercy. Amen.

The congregation joins in as Bilge's mentor guides the candidate down the aisle toward the three stations of discipleship. Three questions will emphasize the cost.

The first station has a worshiper with a cup of dirt.
Turgay asks, "This journey is hard physically. Are you sure you want to continue?"
Bilge answers, "I am sure," and touches the dirt.
Turgay turns to the congregation: "Are you witnesses?"
The congregation responds with one voice, "Yes, we are."
Turgay begins to sing, "O Lord, help."

---

1. All Saints Moda (ASM) practices baptism by pouring (also known as infusion). The 1878 edifice has no baptistry.

The second station has a worshiper with a cup of water.

Turgay asks, "Are you ready to walk with Christ and be tested mentally?"

Bilge responds, "I am ready," dipping fingertips into the water.

Turgay turns to the congregation: "Are you witnesses?"

The congregation responds, "Yes, we are."

Turgay chants, "O Lord, have mercy."

The third station has a worshiper with a lit candle.

Again, Turgay asks, "This journey is difficult spiritually. Are you sure you want to walk this path?"

Bilge responds, "I am sure," and touches the candle flame.

Turgay turns to the congregation: "Are you witnesses?"

The congregation responds, "Yes, we are."

Turgay entreats one last time, "Lord, have mercy. Lord, have mercy. Amen."

The mentor then guides Bilge toward the front altar.

There, a lit *Jesus candle*[2] is positioned in a tall candleholder near the altar rail.

Bilge puts on a long white robe and is handed a candle.

He then lights his from the Jesus candle, signifying a commitment to reflect Jesus Christ.

It's now time to celebrate!

Turgay raises his arms high, waving his hands as he begins to sing.

The congregation picks up the refrain, clapping their hands and singing:

HALLELU, HALLELU, HALLELU, HALLELUJAH

Praise ye the Lord! (author unknown)[3]

What is going on here? Worship events as described above necessitate a multidisciplinary approach that sheds light on ethnographic phenomena from several different angles, including the Christian faith, music, and culture. In this chapter, I review the missiological and theoretical literature that drove my investigation. It helped me unfold the multiplex of dynamics

2 A metaphoric object that represents Jesus, the Light of the world.

3. Whittaker, field notes, 2013–2015.

at work in ASM, a missional church seeking to know God in worship and witness through musico-liturgical inculturation.

Inculturation, a comprehensive term expressing the relationship between gospel and culture, refers to the dynamic translation of the gospel into the culture of local churches. At the core, the implicit and intuitive process of inculturation is a search for identity. As Laurenti Magesa argues, "The gospel as proclaimed in the particular circumstances forces the culture to rediscover itself in its values, language, symbols, and metaphors and to compare and weigh them against it."[4] ASM's inculturation is best considered within the framework of ethnomusicology, which takes place at the intersection of four domains in global church music. See Figure 1.

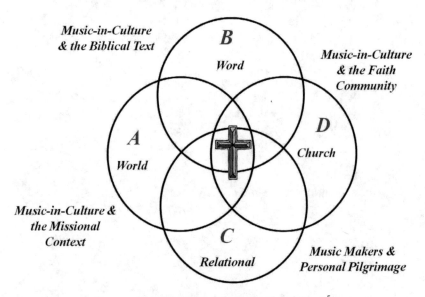

Figure 1: Matrix for Global Studies in Church Music[5]

Roberta King's interactive frame comprises the missional context, the music maker, the faith community, and the biblical text. In this case study, I argue that the study of Turgay Üçal's life, songs, and liturgical worship practice serves as an archetypal investigation relating to the ethnomusicology framework. It demonstrates why and how All Saints Moda's musico-liturgical inculturation is effective, addressing the impact of indigenous

4. Magesa, *Anatomy of Inculturation,* loc. 3307.

5. King, "Beginnings," 13.

Christian music and other aspects of the liturgy on the identity and spiritual formation of the ASM assembly in Istanbul, Turkey.

MISSIONAL CONTEXT (WORLD)

> The concept of culture is . . . the anthropologist's most significant contribution to the missionary endeavor.[6]

It is commonly understood that cultural anthropology is essential for missions,[7] however, many missionaries sent out today are inadequately trained in this cross-cultural foundational discipline . . . or, deliberately ignore its importance. Based upon what I experienced for ten years in the Protestant churches of Turkey (2004–2017), outside of ASM, I have seen little to no indication of this training as it applies to the area of worship. Unaware that anthropological insights are basic to effective cross-cultural communication—particularly as it concerns a people's music—the majority of missionaries have introduced a foreign gospel with Western texts and tunes that marginalize local music and worship forms. For example, Turkey is known worldwide as the bridge between the East and West. Yet, instead of finding both points of contact within people's perspectives and musical needs when planting an evangelical church, the common practice of missionaries has been to introduce what is referred to as the "universal pop aesthetic,"[8] the common pop and rock music styles of North America and Europe.

Most church music in Turkey has come from foreign communicators. The Protestant church is around forty years old, and 60 percent of church leaders are foreigners. While translated Western songs are the primary musical source for worship in both urban and rural areas, a few local and regional hybrid styles are happening with some consistency as well, primarily in the folk genre. But sadly, the growth of the church has been slow.

Much of the foreign music performed in Christian fellowships in Istanbul inadequately communicates the gospel message to those who have never heard it. Why? The exported worship songs are in pop or rock styles, very different from what 'locals' associate with songs of devotion, whether Islamic, Orthodox, or Jewish. The music does not touch the hearts of those that have chosen to hold to the traditional ways and music

6. Luzbetak, *Church and Cultures*, 59.
7. Hiebert, *Anthropological Reflections on Missiological Issues*, 9.
8. Frith, "Introduction," 2.

inherent in their culture. Assessing a similar situation among the Digo people on the Kenyan coast, King writes,

> Western Christian hymns appear to be far from their own world-view perspectives and musical needs. What are the implications for effective evangelization through the use of culturally appropriate music that will speak within their world of cultural patterns?[9]

My response? Conversion should not de-culturize a convert.

Realizing that something has gone wrong, one veteran worker in Turkey recently rang alarm bells with this warning: "The struggle for cultural relevance in Turkey may be won or lost in the music that MBB churches choose to sing."[10] New converts require worship music that will speak within their worldviews and musical styles, enhancing and clarifying the gospel message as they participate in the church within the powerful thrust of the *missio Dei*.

Missio Dei and Music

The theological assumptions reinforcing the concept of *missio Dei* in this study are within the scope of Paul Hiebert's argument that "a theology of missions must begin with God, not humans."[11] I assume mission as belonging to God. Mission is empowered and guided by God himself; we are only participants. Therefore, I also assume that through indigenous music and worship arts, the triune God sends a message that is deeply emotive in any given culture, reaching the place where faith resides. Similarly, a major aspect of worship rites in Turkish is mysticism, to which I turn next.

Mysticism in Turkish Culture

What does mysticism have to do with the musico-liturgical inculturation of ASM's worship practice? How do they relate? The flame of mysticism in Turkey burns brightly and is fanned by the three Abrahamic faith traditions. When the All Saints Moda community gathers to worship, we find unmistakable components of each one. I analyze these components below.

9. King, "Pathways in Christian Music Communication," 9.

10. Clark, "Turkish *Halk* Worship Music," 1.

11. Hiebert, *Anthropological Insights for Missionaries*, 17.

KABBALAH

Starting with Jewish mystical experiences that have been a part of Judaism almost since the beginning, the general term for Jewish mysticism is *kabbalah*. While many Christians consider *kabbalah* dangerous (or deceptive), others have pointed out that there are dual forms of *kabbalah*: those occultic in nature and those that invoke Christian discussions. For example, Turgay employs *kabbalah's* terminology for the laws of development that consist of four levels: inanimate, vegetative, animate, and human[12] to explain spiritual growth. Because Turkey is a society with an oral culture, Turgay finds those particularly useful for transmitting Christian principles and values.

EASTERN ORTHODOXY

Different from the attributes and practices of *kabbalah*, the mystical tradition of the Eastern church ranges from *Lectio Divina*[13] to sensory experiences and ascetic practices to ecstasies and miracles. A sensory application Turgay has borrowed from this stream is the use of incense in the ASM sanctuary before every worship event. Just as in the Eastern church practice, the smoke symbolizes the prayers of the assembly rising into the heavens before God and the ambiance of the heavenly worship (Revelation 8:3–4). Incense also adds a sense of solemnity to worship and helps facilitate entry into the presence of God.

A second nod to the mystical tradition—this time directly related to creativity—is Turgay's practice of *Lectio Divina*. Lyrics and melodies often come spontaneously during worship, the reading of the Word, or meditation and prayer. In the midst of this ancient practice, Turgay has been inspired to create the worship songs and liturgical responses used at ASM.

SUFISM

Tasawwuf, or Sufism, primarily defines mysticism in Turkey. This practice stems from the hunger for transformational experiences with God, who is considered distant and indifferent in Islam. However, while looking into the practice of Sufism, I discovered that it is more complex than originally thought. Over the past twenty years, Sufism has morphed into one of the main interests in the history and social sciences of Islamic studies,

---

12. Laitman, *Basic Concepts in Kabbalah*, 41.

13. A traditional spiritual practice of Scripture reading, meditation, and prayer.

separate from the obscure philosophies and the secret orders such as Mevlevi and Naqshbandi that hold to them.

Corroborating this finding, historian Alexandre Papas claims, "Sufism includes the involvement of mysticism in worldly concerns that is not only in political, legal, and theological issues but also in, among other things, rituals, intellectual productions, fine arts, material culture, and social facts."[14] It affects public arenas through the popularity of mystical poetry and music. In other words, the culture of Sufism—which began in the thirteenth century—is integrated into the very fabric of Turkish society.[15]

Given the triple religious amalgamation that has formed and matured Turgay's life, one can understand how his ministry has tinges of mysticism. Still, my observation is that Turgay carefully holds the mystery of God in harmony with the basic tenets of Christianity. The cultural elements assimilated into the ASM liturgy have weathered a critical contextualization process,[16] and do not open the door to syncretism.

Two Traditions of Turkish Literature

Fundamental to Anatolian culture is a significant history of holy man figures. Examples include the following: local *imam* (mosque leader/preacher) and *muezzin* (vocalist who calls Muslims to prayer) in Sunni Islam, the *dervish* (dancer) and *sheikh* (leader) of the Mevlevi order, and the *dede (cem* ceremony leader/teacher) *and zakir-aşık-ozan* (different names for a *dervish* musician-minstrel) of the Alevi-Bektashi Sufi community. The most famous authors are the Sufi mystics and poets Mevlana Celaddiin-i Rumi[17] and Yunus Emre, of the Mevlevi and Alevi-Bektashi Sufi orders, respectively. Their lyrical themes encompass encounters with God, love, and the deepest parts of human consciousness.

Thirteenth-century contemporaries, Rumi and Emre settled in the same region of Anatolia. Rumi wrote his collection of songs and stories primarily in the literary Persian language for the well-educated urban group of Sufis. Emre, on the other hand, moved among the very poor and performed his songs in the Turkish language of the common people. His songs were orally communicated and not written down until much later. By the middle of the thirteenth century, the formal qualities of the two poetic styles—the

14. Papas, "Toward a New History of Sufism," 82.

15. Wolper, *Cities and Saints,* 16–38.

16. Hiebert, "Critical Contextualization," 104–12.

17. Ciabattari, "Why is Rumi the Bestselling Poet in the US?," lines 32–36.

oral and written—had separated into two camps. The poetic meters in the folk poetic tradition were quantitative (syllabic) as opposed to the qualitative verse used in the written poetic tradition.[18] Additionally, the basic structural unit of folk poetry became the quatrain rather than the couplets more commonly used in written poetry.

Where is this recap of the Turkish poetry evolution leading to, and what has it to do with the worship music of ASM? Simply put, Turgay's songs in *şarkı* form combine elements from both traditions. He composes his works in the literary, poetic couplet-style of Rumi and the Turkish language of Emre. With a father who was an avid reader and writer of Turkish poetry, early in life Turgay became well acquainted with the works of both authors.

Şarkı, an Ideal Love Song Genre

> *Şarkı.* A common form in Turkish music. It is a short vocal form. It is the most frequently used form in Turkish music. It is an equivalent to lied in Western music. It is an equivalent to *türkü* in Turkish folk music.[19]

A brief definition of *şarkı* summarizes a complex meaning that the *sarkı* form entails.[20] The proximity between lied (the West) and *türkü* (Anatolia, or the East) situates *sarkı* as the expression of Istanbul, a convergence between these two worlds. The song genre first became popular during the seventeenth century among court poets and musicians that sang them to the accompaniment of the traditional *bağlama*.[21]

Since then, this song genre has risen above all levels in the Ottoman and modern Turkish society—the religious, economic, ethnic and regional—and has succeeded in surviving the most turbulent changes in Turkish society and cultures. As Klaser notes, "The *şarkı* is a song type well known today as the representative genre of light classical Turkish music performed in the urban

---

18. Holt et al., *Cambridge History of Islam* 2B, 691.

19. Öztüna, "Şarkı." In *Büyük Türk Müsik Mûsikîsi Ansiklopedisi*, 2:332.

20. Klaser, "From an Imagined Paradise to an Imagined Nation," 1.

21. A *bağlama* is a long-necked bowl-bodied lute. It is played by Alevi, Kurds, and Turks alike in Turkey. Each ethno-religious group individually claims it as an emblem of identity, but for different reasons.

popular culture of Istanbul."[22] She further writes, "For my teacher and Turkish listeners in general, *şarkı* is the ideal love song."[23]

We cannot underestimate the *şarkı's* importance to this investigation, as it is a popular song form that has been adapted by Turgay for Christian communication purposes, and it is shaping the identity of ASM's worshipers. By using Turkish art music compositions to express love to Christ, Turgay and the multiethnic, multicultural assembly have gained a sense of identity that is both Christian and Istanbuli. This is a new thing: creating a Christian artistic frame in both poetry and music.

Unfortunately, certain factions within the Protestant church in Turkey have raised objections to Turgay's indigenous hymnody, giving voice to the idea that ASM's hymnody smells like Islam. In response to this accusation, I argue that it is important to understand that ASM's worship songs are written in the makam music system used throughout Central Asia, the Middle East, and North Africa by the three Abrahamic faiths: Orthodox Christianity, Judaism, and Islam. It is incorrect to associate makam music solely with Islam.

> Thesis: Not all *şarkı-s* are religiously oriented and not all *non-şarkı-s* are secular oriented.

> Antithesis: All *şarkı-s* smell of Islam.[24]

While I acknowledge that in many cases, *şarkı-s* are performed in Sufism and *non-şarkı-s* are performed in secular settings, that is not always true. It is an oversimplification of the nature of music; it prescribes general classifications to a fluid phenomenon. Music is more complicated than that. I choose to examine how musical diversity and redefinitions of music might lead to richer and more meaningful experiences in Christian worship.

MUSIC MAKERS (PERSONAL PILGRIMAGE)

> Walking up and down the aisle during hymn singing,[25] Turgay may sit for a minute or so in a vacant pew, worshiping with closed eyes. Or he may pat the head of a child and give the little one a

22. Klaser, "From an Imagined Paradise to an Imagined Nation," Abstract.

23. Klaser, "From an Imagined Paradise to an Imagined Nation," 329.

24. Whittaker, field notes, 2013–2015.

25. With the latest version of the ASM prayerbook in his hand: *Vakit İbadeti* (Daily Worship). Istanbul: GDK (2012–2014).

welcoming smile. Given ASM's location among synagogues, mosques, and Orthodox churches, where the practice of children participating in worship is customary, Turgay's sensitivity to children in worship stems from a belief that it is culturally more appropriate for them to sing and worship together with their parents than separately in "children's church."

This section—the spiritual pilgrimage, or relational arena in King's ethnodoxology frame—involves "the study of people making music."[26] With my focus on Turgay—a national church leader within the context of Turkey—I now discuss how he became an instrument of "ongoing transformation in the world,"[27] particularly as related to the country's Protestant Church and autochthonous musics and practices.

Musical Habitus and "Heart Music"

An explicitly musical habitus is a substratum of French sociologist Pierre Bourdieu's concept of habitus. Simply put, habitus describes "who you are today based on your upbringing and the people and situations that have influenced you while growing up."[28] Following this line of thought, Mark Rimmer advocates primary socialization—or early childhood—in the development of musical interests[29] From Rimmer's rationale, it seems safe to assume that the important influences upon a child's growing concept of music greatly depends upon significant others taking active part in music performances as well as whether the child sings or plays a musical instrument rather than simply turning a music product on or off.

Music was a significant part of Turgay's formative years. His grandmother was an amateur singer of Turkish art songs and accompanied herself on the oud for family and friends. After-dinner entertainment often involved the Üçal family gathered around the radio listening to live performances of Turkish classical music on Turkish Radio and Television Corporation (TRT), or Turgay would play around with the oud (ud in Turkish). In brief, the setting was one in which music was both heard and performed, thus creating a traditional musical habitus.

More to the point, musical habitus is an academic term that equates to what ethnodoxologists call "heart music." Ethnodoxologists such as Joan

26. Titon, *Worlds of Music*, xiv.
27. Shenk, *Changing Frontiers of Mission*, 59.
28. Bourdieu, *Logic of Practice*, 86.
29. Rimmer, "Songs in the Key of Life," 50.

Huyser-Honig consider heart music to be "rooted in a particular place, ethnicity, or experience."[30]

Given his background, there was no contest when Turgay spontaneously began writing hymns; the şarkı song form was a natural fit—an outworking of his musical habitus, sociocultural status, and creativity. The şarkı is Turgay's heart music.

Music-Making Forerunners

My research involving Turgay is situated among a particular group of composers and ethnomusicologists who have or currently are communicating Christ through the means of music from within a local non-Western culture. According to Gregory Barz, investigations of the musical individual in ethnographic studies "show the individual as an actor, embodying his or her own culture, and possessing his or her own agency."[31] Researchers interested in the Christian composer often focus their attention on a representative collection of hymns, typically from the standpoint of its dynamic impact on people in worship. Or they focus on theological concepts and aesthetic notions, such as Florencio Segura in Peru[32] and indigenous composers in Asia.[33]

The motivation for creating new songs starts with the desire of composers to worship God with their artistic expressions of praise rising from their languages and cultures in their contexts of worshiping communities. But after that, it often expands into planting the gospel in the fertile artistic soil of the composers' Christian cultural context, sometimes with coterminous musical traditions in an urban musical soundscape. Examples of such approaches include Mdegella in Tanzania,[34] plus Monteiro and Maraschin in Brazil, Lee in Korea, Feliciano in the Philippines, and Sosa in Argentina.[35] Another particular group of composers tend to on one hand emphasize the hopes, dreams, pain, struggles, and oppression and on the other hand focus on the celebration of liberation: Min in China,[36] Appavoo

30. Huyser-Honig, "Ethnodoxology: Calling all Peoples to Worship," line 3.

31. Barz, *Performing Religion*, 158.

32. Chapman, "Florencio Segura," iii.

33. Loh, *Sound the Bamboo*, viii–xix.

34. Barz, *Performing Religion*, 23.

35. Hawn, *Gather into One*, 40–71. The last five composers are discussed here.

36. See https://www/youtube.com/watch?v=xalsaiWejjo for a fifty-minute English-language documentary film on the composer's life and music.

in India,[37] Matsikenyiri in Zimbabwe,[38] along with Kebede and Gabbiso in Ethiopia.[39] Lastly, there are academic-musicians outside cultural-linguistic groups of people who have helped spark creativity among local artists in different aspects of musical activity. They include Chenoweth in Papua New Guinea,[40] Dargie in South Africa,[41] King in Kenya and Ivory Coast,[42] and William Wade Harris in South-Central Ivory Coast.[43] These studies represent a wide ecumenical sweep across the major church music composers and ethnomusicologists in the global church.

The literature I outlined above presents a general view of a music maker. As Nettl notes, "The individual is the agent and recipient of change."[44] In this specific instance, change ripples throughout an entire society, moving from advocates to innovators to the key music maker and subject of this study: Turgay Üçal.

Turgay: A Distinctive Figure in Inculturation

I have titled this investigation *Music and Liturgy, Identity and Formation: A Study of Inculturation in Turkey* for several reasons. Following his conversion, Turgay searched for a Turkish-led assembly in Istanbul where he could feel at home. His repeated cry was "God, how will I live in my environment as a normal local believer in Christ!" Turgay was emerging from the obscurity of the general national identity[45] and a missionary-imbued Protestant church to find his own identity in Turkey's cultural montage. He later co-founded the first Turkish-led Protestant church in Istanbul with young CCC friends.[46]

---

37. Sherinian, "Indigenization of Tamil Christian Music."

38. Hawn, *Gather into One*, 148–88.

39. Kimberlin, "Scholarship and Art of Ashenafi Kebede," 322–34; Balisky, "Songs of Ethiopia's Tesfaye Gabbiso."

40. Chenoweth, "Peoples of Oceania and Their Music," 640–42.

41. Hawn, *Gather into One*, 104–47.

42. King, "Global Church," 133–50.

43. Krabill, "Encounters," 57–79.

44. Nettl, "Harmless Drudge." 176.

45. The Kemalist government of Atatürk perpetuated the myth that "Turkish society is classless, a single organic unit, one nation, one religion, one history . . . [and] downplayed the actual multiethnic, religious, linguistic nature of the country" (Clark, "Turkish *Halk* Worship Music," 3). Differences began to appear after 1946.

46. Üçal, interview, July 8, 2013; D. H., interview, June 19, 2015.

In today's environment of increasing religious discrimination and political suppression, Protestant nationals in Turkey are again facing some of the same identity challenges. But this time Turgay and the independent ASM assembly are well prepared, unlike other Protestant churches in Turkey today, many of which are affiliated with or supported by Western denominational churches or mission organizations. Others are led by church leaders of minority backgrounds (Armenian, Assyrian, and Kurdish), while still others are led by local pastors who, having been educated in the West, possess Western biblical and cultural perspectives.

Over the past thirty-five years, Turgay has discovered new methods that more effectively communicate the gospel, demonstrating the active role he plays in the process of culture change as an initiator. He is a pioneering Christian leader in Turkey and is known for ingenuity and experimentation. As such, he is the type of individual, according to A. Scott Moreau, who is "more likely to make others feel uncomfortable by moving too fast or too far."[47] In Moreau's epistemological scale on which to locate contextualization ministry, the initiator roles (whether insider or outsider) are absolutely key to contextualization, and a cultural insider is the initiator in approximately 66 percent of the examples.[48] Turgay is in this category. On the continuum, he is a pathfinder, an *innovator*.[49]

Innovator

What separates innovative from non-innovative people? Authors Jeff Dyer, Hal Gregersen, and Clayton Christensen found that innovators were more likely to question, observe, network, and experiment—triggering associational thinking.[50] *Associating*—or the ability to make surprising links across multiple arenas—is often an inherent skill for innovators. Here is a key description of Turgay, the visionary who became a music maker and initiated musico-liturgical inculturation in the ASM worship event. His effectiveness as a composer rests on three aspects: The Scriptures, cultural metaphors, and the pathway of a song.

---

47. Moreau, *Contextualization in World Missions*, 191.

48. Moreau, *Contextualization in World Missions*, 190–91.

49. Moreau, *Contextualization in World Missions*, 256–70.

50. Dyer et al., *Innovator's DNA*, loc. 88.

BIBLICAL TEXT (WORSHIP SONGS)

Hymn texts are guideposts to the deeper issues of life and a composer's attempt to harmonize the Christian faith within their cultural contexts. My focus here is on the specific content and understandings about God found in Turgay's currently sung songs. It is my conviction that their lyric theology is a key component of the spiritual formation process in ASM's worship practice.

Lyric Theology

Fulfilling the biblical encouragement and exhortation when it comes to singing God's Word (Eph 5:19; Col 3:16), Turgay's works encompass psalmody, hymnody, and the more sprightly, uplifting songs that do not fit the staider labels of psalms and hymns. His song texts strengthen the believers' faith and renew vision by reminding them of God's bigger story. In this study of Turgay's eighty hymns, we also discover that Turgay makes good use of metaphors.

Metaphorically Speaking

I apply E. W. Bullinger's definition of Metaphor for the purposes of this project, as the word is often misunderstood and mistakenly used as a general term for any figure of speech. In his book, *Figures of Speech Used in the Bible*, Bullinger writes, "A Metaphor is confined to a distinct affirmation that one thing is another thing, owing to some association or connection in the uses or effects of anything expressed or understood."[51]

Robert Schreiter describes metaphors as "central to the functioning of culture texts, especially those . . . that express in a special way the structures of identities."[52] Turgay's frequent use of metaphors supports this claim. His use of Metaphor in song texts reflects his Turkish cultural values and is an important means of helping people to understand and remember. In this way, Turgay helps them see something from multiple perspectives, presenting a vehicle to gain a solid grasp on complex theological concepts.

---

51. Bullinger, *Figures of Speech Used in the Bible*, 735–43.
52. Schreiter, *Constructing Local Theologies*, 69.

41

Part One: Exploring Turkey's East-West Musical Milieu

Complexity of a Song's Effect

Here I offer a brief discussion about the complexity of a song's effect upon the singer or listener and the impact music is capable of providing. To understand the influence of these songs within the ASM faith community—the comprehensive music communication process—one must trace the sequence in which the receptor receives and acts in return to a message.[53] Corroborating this assessment, Ruth Stone argues, "Studying music processually is accomplished by analyzing the transmission and reception components of the interpretive process."[54] What is the central context for this interpretive process?

Hymn singing within the ASM worship event provides a favorable setting for addressing a concern in the dimensions of time and space. Through participation in this communal activity, congregants may contemplate explicit real-life situations in a slower paced type of communication. Roberta King states, "The expanded timeframe allows people to view parts of an action, analyze it, reflect upon it and then make their own decision as to its particular application."[55]

The progress of a Turgay worship song, moving as it does through various communication channels and within the life of ASM congregants, is intricate. Its line is never straight; often convoluted, it may move back and forth—to and fro. As King further states, "At the same time of sending a message, another effect of the song may be that the participants/singers may find that they are singing their own thoughts."[56] Thus, I investigated this process with the help of a theoretical frame that King calls "the pathway of a song."[57]

Pathway of a Song

This theoretical model provides a tool to trace the path of a song within the music communication process, shedding light on its meandering course. The model comprises three collaborative parts: affective, cognitive, and

53. Engel, *Contemporary Christian Communications*, 57.
54. Stone, *Let the Inside Be Sweet*, 34.
55. King, "Pathways in Christian Music Communication," 242.
56. King, "Pathways in Christian Music Communication," 261.
57. King, "Pathways in Christian Music Communication," 241–42.

behavioral, which act together and are not independent of each other. As can be seen in Figure 2, they are reciprocally engaged.[58]

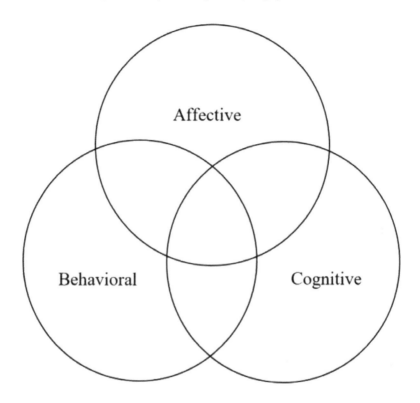

Figure 2: Three Dimensions of the Song Pathway[59]

The *affective* dimension—the most familiar area and where music is initially most influential—is where the pathway of a song begins.[60] It is also where common but deep emotions are touched and attitudes formed, either positive or negative.[61]

58. Bloom, *Taxonomy of Educational Objectives*, 4. This concept model is based on Benjamin Bloom's three domains of learning, although each domain may have had many authors involved in its complete citation. Each particular domain is usually associated with the following primary authors: *affective domain*, David Krathwahl; *cognitive domain*, Benjamin Bloom; and *psychomotor domain*, Anita Harrow.

59. King, "Pathways in Christian Music Communication," 243.

60. King, "Pathways in Christian Music Communication," 241–58.

61. Engel, *Contemporary Christian Communications*," 181.

The *cognitive* dimension—customarily the focus of Christian communicators—is the place where reside beliefs that people hold true.[62] As the essential area to achieve understanding before acting upon life-changing decisions, it is where a hymn communicates its message to the singer. The amalgamation of beliefs, emotions, and total life experiences added to the Word of God within the hymn leads to a period of evaluation. At this crucial point, a decision is made whether or not to apply the message of the song to one's background and circumstances.

The third and final dimension—*behavioral*—concerns the action that follows the period of reflection and decision.[63] For the ASM faith community, worship songs are dynamic and able to effect significant change when the texts speak about God's love, mercy, and power. Moving through and interweaving between these dimensions with great freedom, the Word of God in song is persistent in its pursuit of influence. By employing the pathway of a song's three dimensions, my investigation explains how Turgay's worship songs foster Christian identity and spiritual formation among ASM congregants.[64]

FAITH COMMUNITY (CHURCH)

In the faith community arena of King's approach to Christian ethnomusicology, we consider how people express their belief in God through song. Its role is central to worship, ministry, and mission. Cultural questions are at the center of liturgical thinking. Who a person of faith is, in all respects, reflects the cultural background, including the historical, geographical, and social. There is a wide variety of expressions in liturgical inculturation, ranging from high church liturgies to evangelical seeker services.

In my investigation of ASM's liturgical worship practice, I used a deductive concept-driven approach for building my coding frames in an attempt to reduce the large amount of data collected during the three-year project. This method follows Willms et al.[65] who suggests "starting with some general themes derived from reading the literature and adding more themes and subthemes as you go."[66] This approach led me to the work of two

---

62. King, "Pathways in Christian Music Communication," 259–72.

63. King, "Pathways in Christian Music Communication," 273–81.

64. King, "Pathways in Christian Music Communication," 281–83.

65. Willms et al., "Systematic Approach for Using Qualitative Method," 391–402.

66. Bernard, *Social Research Methods*, 445.

leaders in the field of liturgical studies: Mary McGann and John Witvliet.[67] Below, I detail their respective areas of interest: the role of music in liturgy and liturgical inculturation.

Role of Music in Liturgy

As multiple and far-reaching as the implications of McGann's investigation are, those most applicable to my study have to do with music. Below, I discuss five of them.

1. *The centrality of music to liturgical expressions.* This study is an example of how to explore hymn texts and identify the common theological understandings. It answers the questions of "How?" and "For whom?" In providing a wide-ranging analysis of music in the liturgical worship event at ASM, this study also reveals how deeply rooted music is within the entire liturgical practice.

2. *Liturgical memory and imagination.* McGann's study of liturgical memory and imagination looks at how traditions are being shaped and handed down to future generations. The worship practice of ASM demonstrates a viable option in Turkey: authentic ritual expressions of Christian faith have been united with a historically culturally new and creative dynamism that reflects its East-West context.

3. *A global liturgical theology for the twenty-first century.* As with McGann's work, my investigation pinpoints the need for incorporating fresh perspectives and diverse voices into the liturgical theology conversation. We live in a time of enormous cultural change and greater global awareness. Given the cultural diversity of today, liturgical theology must maintain its importance to the local church's worship experience.

4. *Liturgical collaboration between lay and professional theologians.* While many agree that collaboration in reflective theology is a vital and mutually enriching process, we wonder whether academicians are willing to learn from believers in local cultural traditions such as Turgay's. Will scholars remain tucked away in their ivory towers, or will they attempt to cross-pollinate? As McGann writes, the potential insights promise "a rich harvest for both lay and professional theologians alike and for the rest of the church."[68]

67. "Theological and Conceptual Models," 5–46.

68. McGann, "Interpreting the Ritual Role of Music in Christian Liturgical Practice,"

5. *Implications for training future generations of liturgical scholars.* Years after McGann's work was published, we are still asking the same questions concerning how the liturgical scholars and theologians of the future are being prepared for their role in the church.

> What kinds of methodologies will enable them to undertake a theological task that is inclusive, collaborative, and global at its core?
>
> What cross-disciplinary strategies will equip them to serve the church of the future?
>
> And are we willing to undertake the experimental process by which such questions can be answered?[69]

Good questions to ponder. In the meantime, what are the common themes in liturgical inculturation?

Common Themes in Liturgical Inculturation

While the literature on liturgical inculturation is varied, Witvliet's content analysis of the pertinent literature resulted in identifying the following seven theses.

- Thesis 1: All liturgical action is culturally conditioned.
- Thesis 2: The relationship of liturgy and culture is theologically framed by the biblical-theological categories of creation and incarnation.
- Thesis 3: Liturgical inculturation requires theologically informed cultural criticism of one's own cultural context.
- Thesis 4: The extremes of either complete identification with or rejection of a given culture are to be avoided at all costs.
- Thesis 5: Liturgical action must reflect common elements in the Christian tradition through the unique expressions of a particular cultural context. There must be a judicious balance of particularization and universality.
- Thesis 6: This balance of particularization and universality requires "a mediating strategy" for liturgical contextualization.

244.

69. McGann, "Interpreting the Ritual Role of Music in Christian Liturgical Practice," 241–44.

- Thesis 7: The constituent liturgical actions of the Christian church—including proclamation of the Word, common prayer, baptism, and Eucharist—are among the "universal" or common factors in the Christian tradition.[70]

Each of these theses is reflected in this study. Turgay's application of musico-liturgical inculturation to ASM's worship event focuses on the nature and extent of reformed liturgy and the best "dynamic equivalent"[71] metaphors to describe it. Through Turgay's dedicated leadership, the process of musico-liturgical inculturation thrives at ASM.

The first point to note about inculturation is that we are talking about pluriformity, or diversity, in Christian worship practice, adapting the one unchanging faith to the multiple cultural traditions of the people. The wider perspective of inculturation includes both worship practice and evangelization:

> Liturgical inculturation, viewed from the side of the liturgy . . . may be defined as the process of inserting the texts and rites of the liturgy into the framework of the local culture . . . It means that liturgy and culture share the same pattern of thinking, speaking, and expressing themselves through rites, symbols, and artistic forms. In short, the liturgy is inserted into the culture, history, and tradition of the people among whom the Church dwells.[72]

Aylward Shorter understands inculturation another way: it is "the on-going dialogue between faith and culture or cultures.[73]" Words such as *localization, contextualization,* and *indigenization* also define the term, all with slightly different nuances in meaning. God's revelation is not exclusively linked to a particular culture, race, or time. Perhaps nothing is as important to the future of the church as this process, as Christians attempt to reach diverse peoples embedded in their diverse cultural contexts.

Ntrie-Akpabi Vincent's observations on the state of inculturation in African churches have some relevance to the situation in Turkey. He notes that the earliest studies of evangelization indicate the following:

---

70. Witvliet, "Theological and Conceptual Models for Liturgy and Culture," 34–45; *Worship Seeking Understanding,* 91–123.

71. Kraft, *Christianity in Culture,* 247–69.

72. Chupungco, "*Liturgical Inculturation: Sacramentals, Religiosity, and Catechesis,*" 30. (The term, "inculturation," came into being as a theological term only in the 1970s).

73. Shorter, *Toward a Theology of Inculturation,* 11.

> Their religious and cultural worldviews were not given due recognition during the evangelization. In other words, the [African] cultural context was considered as inferior and inadequate to serve as the possible fertile ground for evangelization. Christian converts were obliged to forsake their cultural identity . . . This created instability, dualistic attitude and identity crisis among African Christians.[74]

Research confirms that inculturation is a true symbiosis, with the Christian experience transposed (speaking in musical terms) into the local culture. It is an ongoing phenomenon whereby Christ transforms people and purifies the culture through partnership and mutuality. The culture interacts with Christianity in a way that the message is communicated to create an understanding of the gospel. Inculturation liberates non-Western believers from "split-level Christianity" tendencies[75] to live their Christian faith in spirit and truth.

Many accept that "the individual theologian, priest or expert must play a prophetic role in the community, with regard to inculturation."[76] Shorter maintains that by listening to church members and interpreting and refining their understandings of Christ, a pastor and other church leaders "help [their people] to be more and more creative in expressing and living their faith."[77] This archetypal pastoral role is where Turgay excels.

Models of Liturgical Inculturation

Dynamic and fluid, Turgay continues to reformulate the Christian worship experience of the ASM church community into the local culture; he leads liturgical inculturation. In this section, I look at Chupungco's three models of inculturation to analyze the liturgical inculturation process at ASM. The models of inculturation encompass creative assimilation,[78] dynamic equivalence,[79] and organic progression.[80]

---

74. Vincent, "Inculturation as Self-Identification," iii.

75. Hiebert et al., *Understanding Folk Religion: Christian Response to Popular Beliefs and Practices,* 15–29.

76. Shorter, *Toward a Theology of Inculturation,* 62.

77. Shorter, *Toward a Theology of Inculturation,* 62.

78. Shorter, *Toward a Theology of Inculturation,* 44–47.

79. Chupungco, *Liturgical Inculturation,* 37–44.

80. Chupungco, *Liturgical Inculturation,* 47–51.

CREATIVE ASSIMILATION

Sometimes creative assimilation is the only appropriate method, especially as it relates to traditional marriage, death rites, and symbols that add depth and meaning to the church's prescribed liturgies. For example, at ASM, Turgay borrows a cultural element to enhance wedding ceremonies: a request for family and friends' approval of the marriage. With another nod to an Islamic tradition in Turkey, upon request, Turgay creatively assimilates memorial services on the anniversary of a loved one's death, honoring through song, prayer, and tribute, the one who has gone.[81]

DYNAMIC EQUIVALENCE

In the beginning of his public ministry, Turgay existed outside of the circle of how-to-do Western church. He was doing crazy things—or so thought his young CCC Western colleagues.[82] Even then, he was searching for how to worship as a believer in Turkey!

Since then, he has translated or converted the overall meaning of carefully chosen ritual practices from the Abrahamic faiths into the liturgy of the ASM assembly. In so doing, he has captured these rituals for Christ, adapting them to convey Christian meanings to the ASM church community; his process is similar to that which Charles Kraft recommends for developing "dynamically equivalent churchness."[83]

ORGANIC PROGRESSION

Obvious to those who regularly attend ASM is that a variety of liturgies for special occasions—baptisms, weddings, memorial ceremonies, Christmas, Easter, and other Christian celebrations—have emerged, stretching the original liturgy in a variety of directions. There is an unbroken relation between this fixed liturgy and the derivatives ensuing from it. This organic progression may be described as the work of replacing or supplementing

81. This practice replaces one of the basic tenets of faith for a Muslim family in terms of "Torment and Blessing in the Grave," based on the *hadeeth*. See https://islamqa.info/en/197749. Typically, the family offers prayers of supplication (*du'aas*) for the deceased in the grave, asking forgiveness at different stages of trials, as the corpse disintegrates.

82. When university students first began meeting in the Swiss Chapel, participants were required to leave their shoes outside the door and sit ala Turkish style—cross-legged on the floor. This traditional custom was short lived. It was discontinued the Sunday a guitarist's brand-new pair of shoes vanished while he was up front leading worship.

83. Kraft, *Christianity in Culture*, 251.

certain liturgical elements when necessary, resulting in a new shape and wider breadth. It fulfills the distinctive needs of different worship approaches throughout the church year.

SUMMARY AND CONCLUSION

In this chapter, I examined the extant scholarship on musico-liturgical inculturation within the frame of King's matrix for studies in church music. The missional and personal pilgrimage domains reveal the familial, mystical, poetical, and musical influences in Turgay's life and, by extension, his ministry and hymnody. While the Protestant-faith-community domain in Turkey demonstrates the theological foundations for inculturation, as well as the scriptural and church history imperatives for the process, it shows that fruitful models of inculturation have not been well examined or pursued. ASM is an anomaly among Protestant faith communities in Turkey. In terms of the biblical text domain, I used ethnodoxological processes to study Turgay's worship songs. Scriptural content and metaphoric expressions reveal the depth of Turgay's feelings, attitude, and theological understanding of God, while the pathway of a song aid in determining the full effect of his hymnody on the day-to-day living of the ASM faith community.

Consequently, I argue for a correlation between musico-liturgical inculturation, identity, and spiritual formation. The goal is to provide a resource for those who come behind me, so that deep, authentic worship may freely flow within churches locally, as well as around the globe. In the next chapter, I address my research schedule and process, including the research design and methods employed in this study.

3

Itineraries to Meaning

> The use of traveling is to regulate imagination by reality and in-
> stead of thinking how things may be, to see them as they are.[1]

IN THE TWO PREVIOUS chapters, I described the general research context and my theoretical framework for this study. In this chapter, I discuss the overall research process, including the defense of my rationale for the case study research design, the research schedule, and my sample selection and song-sample selection. I then assess my primary research methods, which are followed by a diverse group of secondary methods.

This research is a diachronic embedded case study designed to help me discover the impact of the indigenous songs of a pastor-composer on a church community over the course of several years.[2] I focus on his musico-liturgical inculturation. This study involved me approaching the people, as I needed to know their attitudes toward the new songs, and I needed to gauge how the music affected their daily lives. For these reasons, I placed the case study within a missiological framework: King's four-arena matrix for studies in global church music, which shows how the multifaceted dynamics operate in four musical arenas simultaneously.[3] In Figure 3, we see the framework that guided my research, the data collection methods used within each quadrant, and in two cases (faith community and music maker), some of the actual data collected.

1. Johnson, 1773 letter, website.
2. Yin, *Case Study Research*, 46–66.
3. King, "Beginnings," 13.

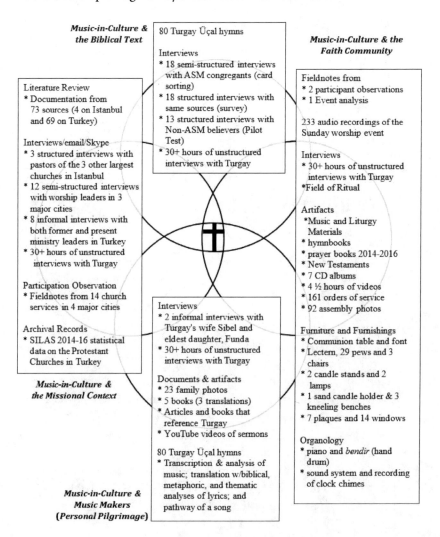

Music-in-Culture & the Biblical Text

80 Turgay Üçal hymns

Interviews
* 18 semi-structured interviews with ASM congregants (card sorting)
* 18 structured interviews with same sources (survey)
* 13 structured interviews with Non-ASM believers (Pilot Test)
* 30+ hours of unstructured interviews with Turgay

Music-in-Culture & the Faith Community

Fieldnotes from
* 2 participant observations
* 1 Event analysis

233 audio recordings of the Sunday worship event

Interviews
* 30+ hours of unstructured interviews with Turgay
*Field of Ritual

Artifacts
*Music and Liturgy Materials
* hymnbooks
* prayer books 2014-2016
* New Testaments
* 7 CD albums
* 4 ½ hours of videos
* 161 orders of service
* 92 assembly photos

Furniture and Furnishings
* Communion table and font
* Lectern, 29 pews and 3 chairs
* 2 candle stands and 2 lamps
* 1 sand candle holder & 3 kneeling benches
* 7 plaques and 14 windows

Organology
* piano and *bendir* (hand drum)
* sound system and recording of clock chimes

Literature Review
* Documentation from 73 sources (4 on Istanbul and 69 on Turkey)

Interviews/email/Skype
* 3 structured interviews with pastors of the 3 other largest churches in Istanbul
* 12 semi-structured interviews with worship leaders in 3 major cities
* 8 informal interviews with both former and present ministry leaders in Turkey
* 30+ hours of unstructured interviews with Turgay

Participation Observation
* Fieldnotes from 14 church services in 4 major cities

Archival Records
* SILAS 2014-16 statistical data on the Protestant Churches in Turkey

Music-in-Culture & the Missional Context

Interviews
* 2 informal interviews with Turgay's wife Sibel and eldest daughter, Funda
* 30+ hours of unstructured interviews with Turgay

Documents & artifacts
* 23 family photos
* 5 books (3 translations)
* Articles and books that reference Turgay
* YouTube videos of sermons

80 Turgay Üçal hymns
* Transcription & analysis of music; translation w/biblical, metaphoric, and thematic analyses of lyrics; and pathway of a song

Music-in-Culture & Music Makers (Personal Pilgrimage)

Figure 3: Research Arenas, Methods, and Data Collected

RESEARCH ARENAS

By approaching the questions in each arena—missional context, music maker, faith community, and biblical text—with multiple methods, I was able to create triangulation and verify the validity of the investigation. These four interactive spheres of study not only served as my research framework but also provided a format for the methods employed and data collected. In each sphere, as relevant, I applied the insights I gained from my thirty-two hours of unstructured interviews with Turgay.

Missional Context (World)

In the *missional context*, I examined the background of the study, in which I attempted to answer the question "What significant events and influences in Turgay's life led to the inception of musico-liturgical inculturation?" A review of the literature about Turkey's sociocultural history and the foreign missionary influence on current worship practice was one of my main research methods (see chapter one). This was supported by interviews with past and present workers/church leaders,[4] in addition to the only two research studies related to Protestant worship music in Turkey,[5] and SILAS 2013–15 archival records.[6]

This research question calls attention to the lacunae in the missional literature of Turkey. Despite the paucity of available literature, I gathered information from "living libraries:" older ministry leaders—both local and foreign—who shared their memories about the early years of Turkey's Protestant church history, starting in the 1980s. This supplemented my structured interviews with worship leaders and the other three pastors of the largest churches in Istanbul (see Appendix D). I completed my data-collecting methods in the missional context with field notes from participant observation at churches in four major cities.

Music Makers (Personal Pilgrimage)

The research arena of the *music makers* concerns the relational aspect, addressing those who make the music within the missional setting. Composers and worship leaders like Turgay play a key role in leading people into God's presence, blending biblical truth, music, and other cultural

---

4. See Appendix D.

5. Clark, "Turkish *Halk* Worship Music;" and Perigo, "Leading a Workshop on Contextual Songwriting."

6. SILAS is a small Christian research organization working alongside the Protestant evangelical association of church leaders in Turkey. It collects and distributes statistical data about the congregations, describing the churches, locations, years established, church sizes, and names of the pastors as well as the number of conversions, baptisms, and changes in religious identity on the national identity cards of converts (public confession of a person's allegiance to Christ in this predominantly Muslim country).

elements to declare God's glory and the redeeming work of Christ on the cross. Through thirty-two hours of in-depth unstructured interviews with Turgay[7] as well as through informal interviews with his family and friends,[8] I inquired about Turgay's background, theology, and ministry, exploring and considering the specific skill sets that are distinctively his and how he chose to employ them.

I also narrowed my focus in this quadrant with respect to Turgay's role as chief music maker, seeking to answer the research question, "What are the key themes in Turgay's eighty-song anthology of indigenous hymns?" Results are detailed in chapter 7 and Appendix I. To understand them, I studied both music and lyrics, and—because I don't speak fluent Turkish— I had the texts translated into English.[9] I wanted to know how Turgay theologizes through the music-making process. Other sources of collected evidence in this quadrant are blogs and articles recounting his ministry, including the books he authored or co-authored,[10] and related photos.[11]

Faith Community (Church)

In the *faith community* research arena, I considered how Turgay's songs contributed to making Christ known and worshiped among the nations with the following question, "What is the role of music in the worship practice of All Saints Moda (ASM)?" (See a detailed discussion of results in chapter 5). This question required the examination of every music-related component in the liturgy, their placement throughout ASM's worship event, and in what ways they communicate the Christian faith. Research methods included two participant observations,[12] an event analysis, mapping of the ritual, and 233 audio recordings of weekly services, together with four and a half hours of video recordings of the Sunday worship practice. Additionally, I examined artifacts, music and liturgy materials, furniture and furnishings, and organology. My unstructured interviews with Turgay also greatly contributed to this portion of the study.

---

7. See Appendix C.

8. See Appendix D.

9. As I explained earlier, the other forty-five songs were previously transcribed.

10. See Appendix A.

11. See Appendix B.

12. I was an active participant in the ASM church assembly for nine years (2008–2017).

Biblical Text (Worship Songs)

In the research arena of *biblical texts*, I looked at the hymn texts in terms of understanding how the ASM community practices a theology of music in context. My quest was to answer the question: "How do Turgay's worship songs affectively, cognitively, and behaviorally impact the everyday lives of participants?" (My findings are detailed in chapters 6 and 7, together with appendices J and K). I conducted structured interviews in a pilot test to evaluate how to do that. I decided I could administer a two-tiered set of interviews with assembly members to help me reach my goal. Those interviews involved a card-sorting activity and a survey.

Having laid out my four-arena research schedule and their corresponding methods and data collected, I turn now to the defense of the research design, my sample selection and song-sample selection, and the evaluation of my varied collection of methods.

RESEARCH DESIGN

The core interpretive frameworks of researchers remain largely invisible. Nonetheless, they serve to guide the research process. I was able to pinpoint the philosophical assumptions, paradigms, and theories that would classify this qualitative study early in the research process. I conducted this study from an ethnographic approach, allowing me to focus on the experiential aspects of a church community's worship practice and how these experiences were interpreted or shared. I looked at what the people did (*behaviors*), what they said (*language*), and what they used (*artifacts*).[13] My mixed method research—a combination of both qualitative and quantitative research techniques—became apparent through inductive reasoning as I collected and assessed the data. How, then, did I choose the research sample for my dissertation?

Sample Selection

The All Saints Moda community embodies a multiplicity of identities. My sample needed to represent a cross-section of the population demographics: gender, age, ethnicity, religious background, and length of time as a believer at ASM. Since I had limited knowledge of those who attended, I approached Jaklin, a church office assistant, to help gather a representative group of people.

13. Spradley, *Participant Observation*, 10.

Part One: Exploring Turkey's East-West Musical Milieu

From a congregation of approximately eighty adults, I selected the initial sample of twenty-two respondents. I met with obstacles in attaining full participation: Two people moved out of the country, and two others discontinued attending ASM within a year's period. As a result, eighteen of the twenty-two respondents took part in both segments of the two-tiered interview process (card sorting and survey). Despite these impediments, the final sample accurately represented the church demographics (see Table 2).

Table 2: Composite Characteristics of Respondents

Gender	Age	Religious Background	Ethnicity	Length of time as a Believer	Length of time at ASM
M—4	20s—3	Sunni Muslim —8	Turks—9	3 yrs or less— 4	3 yrs or less—6
F—14	30s—4	Armenian Ortho—5	Armenians—6	4-10 yrs—3	4-10 yrs—3
	40s—7	Alevi—2	Kurds—2	11-20 yrs—5	11-20 yrs—9
	50s—3	Russian Ortho—2	Russian—1	over 20 yrs—1	
	60s—1	Protestant—1		Since childhood—5	

There was considerable diversity among the participants. The congregants involved fourteen females and four males, more than three times the number of women to men. This gender ratio is typical of Protestant congregations in Turkey, where women outnumber men. The population of the group was almost uniformly distributed across adulthood: participants mostly ranged in age from twenty through fifty. Almost half were in their forties, while the others were correspondingly spread across the twenties, thirties, and fifties. One individual was over sixty. Half of the participants were Muslim background believers (MBBs), while the other half were of Orthodox Christian and Protestant evangelical origins. Half of the congregants were Turks, closely followed in number by Armenians, then Kurds, and one Russian.

The characteristics related to length of time as believers and length of time at ASM have particular relevance to the overall conclusion. For that reason, I will discuss them in the last chapter. In the next section, I discuss my selection of a song sample—a collection of the favorite worship songs among ASM congregants—to investigate how and why Turgay's songs might make a significant difference in the effective communication of Christ.

Song-Sample Selection

The 2013 ten-week cycle of ASM worship music at the time of this research served as the pool from which I drew my song sample (see Appendix G). It contained fifty songs comprised of three genres: twenty-six translated Western (TW), nineteen Turkish *sanat* music (TSM), and five Turkish folk music (TFM). Approaching Jaklin once more for wise counsel, this time in regard to the song sample, I relied on her familiarity with the repertoire and asked her to suggest a variety of favorite worship songs to reflect this diversity. From the collection, I assembled a subset of nineteen song titles (nine TW, nine TMM, and one TFM), about one-third of the total group.[14] My reason for choosing an equal number of TW and TMM genres, despite the twenty-one to fifteen ratio in the ten-week cycle, was directly related to the number of supplementary TMM worship songs that Turgay spontaneously uses each week. A convincing approximation had to be made, taking into account the dynamic aspects of the worship practice.

My cross-section approach allowed me to compare the attitudes of the ASM assembly toward the phenomenon that was taking place within a real-life context. I could see my need for multiple sources of evidence and multiple research approaches in my attempt to unpack the complexity and pervasiveness of the influence of Turgay's indigenous songs on the ASM assembly.

METHODS REVIEW

I conducted both a simultaneous and sequential qualitative mixed method design over a three-year period from mid-2012 to mid-2015 in four cities in Turkey: Istanbul, Diyarbakir, Izmir, and Antalya. Therefore, this case study is diachronic. Table 3 offers a compact look at the full range of evidence I used during this research period and demonstrates how the overlapping and juxtaposed methods fit together as an ensemble approach to interpretive research. The patterns represent the four segments of the research and their occurrences.

14. These nineteen song titles are marked by three asterisks in Appendix G.

Table 3: Research Methods

Methods	2012	2013	2014	2015
Literature Review	▓	▓	▓	▓
Participant Observation	▓	▓	▓	▓
Non-structured Interviews (Turgay)		▓	▓	
Structured Interviews (pilot test)*		▓		
Semi-structured Interviews (card-sorting)		▓	▓	
Structured Interviews (survey)			▓	
Non-structured Interviews (church leaders,			▓	
Transcription and Analysis (music)	▓	▓	▓	▓
Biblical, Metaphoric and Thematic Analyses (lyrics)			▓	▓
Documents, Archival Records, and Artifacts			▓	
Worship Event Analysis				▓
Mapping the Field of Ritual				▓

*Results: Not used, as the test did not fit the criteria

In the following section, I describe my rationale for the twelve methods I used in the research process, including the primary and secondary methods, plus my strategies for answering the research questions.

Primary Methods

The two main research methods used in this study involved participant observation and interviews. Participant observation is one of the most common techniques for collecting qualitative data. "It is a way of "experiencing the lives of the people you are studying as much as you can."[15] While this method may be considered problematic because of its manipulative leanings, it was essential for shedding light on the four research questions. Chatting with congregants over cups of hot tea after church services and events was instrumental in building trust.

I later opted for active participation observation, involving myself not only in church-related activities and in my specific formal role as researcher, but also in sharing in the lives of those observed on a personal level. In visits with ASM women friends and in social outings with my husband and other married couples in the assembly, I gained insights into the workings of the church community that I would not have had otherwise. D. L. Jorgensen would agree. He claims that participant observation offers possibilities for the researcher on a continuum, from being a complete outsider to being a complete insider.[16] Active participation observation helped ensure

---

15. Bernard, *Social Research Methods*, 319.

16. Jorgensen, *Participant Observation*, 55.

my data quality. Further, respondents were more apt to respond positively to my request for the two back-to-back research interviews.

Early on, I recognized the problem related to this method: the risk of biased data, based on my support of the people in this case study. As I sought to understand how ASM believers thought and felt about their world, I became emotionally involved, yet I was also mindful of the research requirement to observe without losing objectivity. How was I to avoid the trap of seeing progressive change through musico-liturgical inculturation that was not real or as optimistic as I would have anticipated?

While bias is often present in a study, strong scientific research requires that the researcher adhere to accepted paradigms with a self-reflection that governs the collected data. While these measures are not infallible, by using them, I was able to reduce the probability of arbitrary bias and construct greater validity and reliability.

As with participant observation, the interview is an indispensable data-collecting method in qualitative research. Interviews capture the perspectives behind the participants' experiences. Within the context of my case study, the most important component of the interviews was language, since all events were in Turkish. In my attempt to understand the meaning of the ASM song lyrics or liturgy, I frequently asked informal questions starting with the words *what* or *why*. Impromptu interviews often followed participation observation, triggered by what I heard and saw or when I approached people at social events to ask more incisive questions. By checking with multiple informants, I was careful to avoid bias and errors. I also tried to not extrapolate my beliefs or treat favorably the information that supported what I believed or wanted to believe.

Unstructured interviews conducted within the music-maker arena dealt with Turgay's life story and enabled me to enter his world. The idea of the unstructured interview "is to get people to open up and let them express themselves in their own terms and at their own pace," according to H. Russell Bernard.[17] It was a great fit for my research.

Turgay fully engaged in the interviews, describing his life course stages—including his journey to Christ—pastoral ministry experiences, and music-making activities in a coherent order, while sharing stories along the way. Our interviews developed into a type of pattern. After a short discussion on the topics of the day, I switched on the recorder, announced the date and Turgay's name, and began to listen. Taking notes

---

17. Bernard, *Social Research Methods*, 191.

now and again, I seldom interrupted but asked questions when I needed clarification or deeper insight.

I could not have selected a better method than the subjective narrative of the life story to help me understand Turgay from the insider's point of view, because I was conducting long-term research and was able to interview him multiple occasions on his own turf in the church office. My interviews with Turgay totaled thirty-two hours and were supplemented with follow-up emails.

In the process, I discovered that I had to ask myself some hard questions on ethical issues, because I was conducting life story interviews with a real person and I was attempting to assist him in telling his story for a larger audience. Mindful that interpretive biography research is perceived as "blurring the lines between fact and fiction" because biographies are, in a sense, written autobiographies of the writers.[18] I needed to be certain in the post-interview stage of my collaboration that I had effectively and efficiently interpreted Turgay's experience.

Although not fail-safe, the measures I used involved supplemental interviews with former colleagues and current ministry leaders across Turkey to corroborate Turgay's insights and to search for contrary evidence as a way of reducing arbitrary bias. See Appendix D for church leader interview references.

In my focus on understanding the effect of Turgay's music on ASM congregants and its ability to touch people at the deepest level, I needed to explore peoples' attitudes toward the songs. Did the music impact them? If so, how?

My questioning route with respondents in the Music-in-Culture and the Biblical Text arena was a result of what I had learned through the pilot test. By "sequencing the questions" through a two-tiered set of interviews,[19] I implemented a special kind of research procedure known as *funneling*, which means asking from general to specific, from broad to narrow. The procedure involved semi-structured interviews (card sorting) followed by structured interviews (survey). Card sorting was based on a semi-structured interview guide, providing access to topics that needed to be covered in a particular order and handled face-to-face.[20] This effective first step in grasping how the church community thought and felt about the two genres

18. Creswell, *Qualitative Inquiry and Research Design*, 50.
19. Cohen and Manion, *Research Methods in Education*, 277.
20. Bernard, *Social Research Methods*, 191.

of music (Turkish and Western) used at ASM was followed by a survey that gauged people's attitudes toward Turgay's worship songs, the meaningfulness of the music, and how it worked in their lives. I considered these methods helpful for fully grasping how the ASM community felt about the content and music genres they sing each week: translated Western songs (TW), Turkish makam music (TMM),[21] and Turkish folk music (TFM). How did the respondents perceive similarities and differences among these genres? (See Appendix J for the card-sorting protocol).

My structured interviews (survey), which I kept to an interview schedule, were more restrictive than the semi-structured interviews (card sorting). The original plan was to conduct two or three focus groups, with the goal of determining how Turgay's worship songs affectively, cognitively, and behaviorally impacted the ASM participants. As Judith Bell argues,

> It is therefore not enough simply to naively observe what a person is doing or how they are behaving within any given situation. In order to understand what is actually going on within that situation it is necessary to understand the meanings of the actions, the way the situation is being interpreted by those performing within it and the reasons behind the ways individuals and communities act in the particular ways that they do.[22]

But my efforts to arrange focus group meetings simply did not work in Istanbul. Why? Istanbul was the metropolis that "rose to the top spot in the world in terms of traffic congestion in 2014,"[23] plus it was impossible to form these groups when respondents were scattered over such a large geographical area. Providentially, I was able to gather the indispensable data another way. I engaged a respected young man in the congregation (and Christian university grad) to help carry out the interviews on a one-to-one basis.

At the outset, I trained O. J.[24] in the objectives of the structured interview. He served as translator and observed as I conducted the first interview. Having adapted a focus group protocol created by King[25] into a survey, I was able to provide answers to research questions such as "How

21. Ottoman-Turkish makam music: classical Turkish music and Turkish *sanat* music.

22. Bell, *Doing Your Research Project*, 5.

23. TomTom International BV (Amsterdam) analyzes traffic congestion in more than two hundred cities around the world.

24. Given the security risks of publicly identifying as a Christian in Turkey, O. J. and several interviewees chose to be identified by their initials instead of their names.

25. King, "Pathways of Christian Music Communication," 353–54.

did the hymns impact your life?" and "How did the hymns influence your decisions and lifestyle?" I probed in order to deepen the response and to increase the richness of the acquired data. When my assistant was ready, he conducted the remaining interviews by means of two standard research procedures: face-to-face and by telephone (See Appendix K for the survey question guide and responses). In addition to the primary research methods, I employed secondary methods to help bridge the two types and to address the nature of the research problems and approach.

Secondary Methods

My secondary methods encompassed the following eight items: literature review, musical transcription and analysis; content analyses of Turgay's song texts (Scripture, metaphor, and theme); event-centered analysis of the liturgy, and mapping the field of ritual, as well as documents, archival records and artifacts.

Transcription has long been an essential practice in ethnomusicology and anthropology. I transcribed thirty-five worship songs, notating two aspects of a song's musical style: pitch (notes) and duration (length of pitches) in the audio coding of Turgay's hymnody. This procedure was followed by three types of lyric content analysis: biblical, metaphoric, and thematic.

The next method I used in this study—event-centered analysis—was drawn from ritual studies and adapted for the goals of this research. This method helped to understand the meanings interwoven into ASM's liturgy. As described by Catherine Bell, a liturgy is "the means by which collective beliefs and ideals are simultaneously generated, experienced, and affirmed as real by the community."[26] Liturgy has the power to shape a believer's Christian beliefs and behavior. In a related examination of the broader context of the worship milieu, I used Ronald Grimes's "mapping the field of ritual" framework.[27] His six categories of questions encompass space, objects, time, sound and language, identity, and actions.

Lastly, in addition to gathering accompanying documents, archival records, and artifacts, this research project included a personal tour of Mudanya (Turgay's hometown) in 2014, led by Turgay and his wife, Sibel. There, I was privileged to meet his parents and interview his eldest daughter, Funda, who live in the small city. The applied ethnomusicology component of this study reveals Turgay's ultimate goal of developing

26. Bell, *Ritual Theory, Ritual Practice*, 20.
27. Grimes, *Beginnings in Ritual Studies*, 19–32.

culturally appropriate worship songs for effective communication in all areas of church ministry.

SUMMARY

In this chapter, I discussed the overall research design, philosophical paradigm, and research process. I presented my rationale for the embedded case study, describing the sample, song-sample, along with primary and secondary data-collection methods that correspond to the four arenas in King's ethnodoxology matrix, and I defended my choice of methods. I addressed potential investigator bias along with the validity and reliability I built into the study design. I achieved triangulation through the mixed-method approach: the use of an assortment of collaborative methods and data-collection resources. From here, I move to an overview of Turgay's life.

Turgay Üçal, Agent of Change

4

Personal Pilgrimage

IN THIS CHAPTER, I examine Turgay Üçal's background in order to gain a more complete picture of his life. Of interest is the importance of tight family and community connections that deeply impacted him. I describe Turgay's early music inclinations, his journey to Christ, the context of his discipleship, his first ministry positions, his first music making experience, and his gifting as prophet and priest.

Over the last few years, there have been a growing number of ethnomusicological studies that focus on the lives of individual persons. Examples that illustrate this trend within the discipline and are similar to mine include Zoe Sherinian's study of James Theophilus Appavoo in India (1998), Deborah Chapman's treatment of the contextualization of evangelical songs by Florencio Segura in Peru (2006), Swee-Hong Lim's appraisal of the pioneering work of I-to Loh in Asia (2008), and Lila Balisky's study in Ethiopia of poet/soloist Tesfaye Gabbiso and his songs (2015). These treatises cover a broad sweep of geographical work and a range of contrasting musical lives, yet each of the authors concentrates on the music of an indigenous composer and his local theology.

My data analysis and representation of the biography tradition of inquiry is based upon Norman Denzin[1] and John Creswell.[2] I used qualitative content analysis (QCA), known as the best method for describing and summarizing the main areas of narrative texts. Creswell suggests that once life events are mapped out, stories and epiphanies will rise from the

1. Denzin, *Interpretive Interactionism*, 56–69.
2. Creswell, *Qualitative Inquiry and Research Design*, 148–49.

interviews, "the individual's biography is reconstructed, and the researcher identifies factors that have shaped the life."[3] I found this to be true in my experience. I also had the first sub-question in mind as I read, and so I read for a purpose: "What significant events and influences in Turgay's life led to the inception of musico-liturgical inculturation?" As the logical starting point, I begin by tracing his upbringing and the process of his conversion to Christianity.

EARLY LIFE

Born in 1962, Turgay spent his first four years in the seaside city of Mudanya, along the southern shore of the Sea of Marmara in Turkey. The small city (at that time, around six thousand inhabitants) is known for its olive oil and a harbor used by local fishing and cargo boats. Here, his parents, grandparents, relatives, and friends nurtured him and helped him to become an individual who was focused and positive, with a strong sense of self-esteem.[4] When Turgay was five years old, his newly retired army officer father moved the family to the metropolitan city of Istanbul, ninety minutes north by seabus (see map 3).

---

3. Creswell, *Qualitative Inquiry and Research Design*, 146–47.

4. Funda (Turgay's eldest daughter), interview, July 30, 2014. She credits this information to her grandparents who never tired of sharing stories about her father's childhood with her.

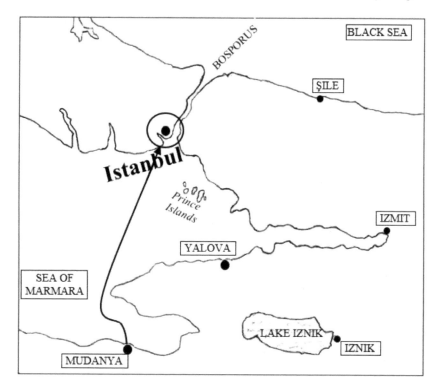

Map 3: Mudanya to Istanbul

Turgay's exceptionalism was apparent early on, including his creative tendencies and spiritual sensitivities. With a preference for adult conversation, his early influences flowed organically. Describing his artistic habitus—in the terms of the French sociologist Pierre Bourdieu[5]—Turgay reveals that his father wrote poetry and his maternal grandmother, who died before he was born, often sang *şarkı-s* (Turkish art songs). She accompanied herself on the oud, a short-neck lute-type, pear-shaped traditional stringed Turkish instrument.

The bourgeois family enjoyed listening to radio broadcasts of Turkish classical music, a favorite form of evening entertainment. This exposure to traditional music was facilitated by the state-owned Turkish Radio and Television Corporation (TRT) and the rebroadcasting of Turkish classical music during the 1970s, years after the Turkish government's music reforms of 1934–36 that attempted to ban it from the radio airwaves. Turgay's love for

5. Bourdieu, *Logic of Practice*, 86.

traditional music is not surprising. He also enjoyed playing around with the oud. Later in school, he became familiar with European classical music. At ease thereafter with two different music systems, Turgay established a viable currency in music. This acquisition of bicultural and bi-musical capacity in his youth prepared him for things he never could have imagined.

JOURNEY TO CHRIST

Spiritual conversion often requires extended time. This is true of Turgay's conversion experience. A sequence of significant events changed a shifting pattern into a linear progression of sin, salvation, and assurance.[6] The multiple factors contributing to Turgay's faith in Christ came to light in our first interview, since his spiritual journey began in childhood.

Perhaps surprisingly, the stance of Turgay's non-religious parents— very much in step with the ideals established in the secular Republic—was lost on him. Instead, he was greatly impacted by the piety of his "moderate-Muslim" grandmother, who instilled in him belief in a sovereign God.[7] During summer visits in Mudanya, he remembers sitting or kneeling by her side throughout the *namāz*, a physical, mental, and spiritual ritual prayer observed by pious Muslims five times daily at prescribed times. Turgay also attended weekly classes at the local mosque with an imam who had high hopes that Turgay would become a religious leader. Turgay grew up with the voices of Qur'an reciters echoing in his ears.

Turgay recalls other memories of the family's idyllic neighborhood in Istanbul where they settled. He observed,

> It was like the end of the Ottoman-time type of families there— the very old-fashioned Turkish families. We had a wonderful family relationship with neighbors loving each other. They were like my relatives. If my mother wasn't at home, I went to a neighbor, knocked on the door, and ate dinner there. I lived a kind of communal life.[8]

Listening to Turgay's recollections of his early influences, I sensed that he cherished family, his traditional upbringing, and culture. Unfortunately, his idyllic life was about to disappear.

6. Others who have commented on Turgay's conversion experience include Carnes, "Jesus in Turkey," 25; Pikkert, "Protestant Missionaries to the Middle East: Ambassadors of Christ or Culture?" 272; and Bultema, "Muslims Coming to Christ in Turkey," 27–31.

7. Üçal, interview, July 8, 2013.

8. Üçal, interview, July 8, 2013.

Toward the end of the 1970s, Turkey experienced a political maelstrom, with Communist leftists, Fascist rightists, and fundamentalist religious groups all at war with each other. Turgay was in middle school and then secondary school during this time, and the anxiety he felt in the midst of this turmoil on the streets of Istanbul contributed to his growing interest in spiritual matters. Deep inquisitiveness marked his capabilities as an emerging critical thinker. When Turgay was fifteen, he began to read the Qur'an. He doesn't remember much about the content, except that he became curious about why Jesus didn't die. This curiosity was the first of three factors that led him to consider Christianity.

Turgay remembers that as he began processing the question of why Jesus did not die, he became attuned to an awareness of its implications. During that same year, a homework reading assignment of Victor Hugo's book *Les Miserables* and a classic American TV show piqued his curiosity. In *Les Miserables*, while a guest in the home of a priest, the protagonist Jean Valjean wrestles with the concepts of sin and forgiveness. The forgiveness the priest extends to Jean Valjean became the second factor that caught Turgay's attention.

Turgay was walking a unique path to Christ. There was only one Turkish channel on a black-and-white TV at the time, and "Little House on the Prairie" came on every Saturday. Turgay never missed an episode, and watching Laura Ingalls and her family talking with God touched his heart. Who could have guessed that "Little House on the Prairie" would serve as an early mass media tool of evangelism?

On the day Turgay's initial step toward Christianity occurred, he noticed the only bookstore in Istanbul selling Bibles, Bible Society Bookshop, situated on Istiklal Avenue, one of the busiest streets in the city. He remembers walking back and forth to make sure no one he knew was around. With fear and trepidation, Turgay entered the shop and purchased a New Testament. He tried reading the New Testament, imitating what he saw on "Little House on the Prairie," but he did not understand the Bible's meaning.[9] He needed outside help.

Shortly after that, Turgay started attending the St. Antoine Catholic Church, just up the street from the bookshop, which was run by Italian priests. He began asking questions. The priests were kind to him but wary. Turgay was underage, only sixteen years old. It was illegal for Christians to proselytize underage Muslims. Afraid of being arrested and thrown in jail,

9. Üçal, interview, July 8, 2013.

one of the priests tried to discourage Turgay from becoming a seeker. All efforts failed. Turgay showed up at the church every day, helping out in the office with the printing of the church's monthly publications on a hand-operated printing machine, while learning whatever he could about this faith. He considered becoming Catholic. But the priests often conversed in Italian, and their culture was different, too.

Around the same time, Turgay discovered a small group of Armenians, Syrian, and Greek Protestants meeting in the basement of the church.

> I didn't know the difference between Catholic and Protestant because of my Muslim background. I thought Christianity was Christianity. So, when I heard the sermon in garbled Turkish and their strange music accompanied with loud singing and hand clapping, it seemed really odd to me.[10]

Regardless, Turgay joined the worshippers downstairs from time to time, desiring to learn more about Christ. The Armenian people were "very good people—wonderful people," as he fondly recalled. Again, the culture became challenging for the sixteen-year-old Turgay. He remembers,

> Their terminology did not make sense to me. For example, "The blood of Jesus cleanses me!" Oh, my goodness! It was very bloody and very complicated. I noticed that the Protestants were criticizing the Catholic theology, and the Catholics were criticizing the Protestant theology. It was a difficult situation for me. I was really confused. In mosques, I never heard theological disputes. Christianity appeared very complicated.[11]

The church leaders were oblivious of their contentious attitudes and the impact on this vulnerable teenager. Turgay had picked up on the tension between the two Christian denominations and their unbridled animosity toward each other. In 1979, it came to a head when the Protestants approached Turgay about making a decision:

> "If you are a Christian, you have to be baptized. Do you believe in Christ?"
> Turgay responded, "Yes, I believe."
> And they said, "Okay, we'll baptize you in the name of Jesus."[12]

10. Üçal, interview, July 8, 2013.
11. Üçal, interview, July 8, 2013.
12. Üçal, interview, July 8, 2013.

Turgay was young in his faith and did not question them. He simply went along. He was unaware of the meaning of the baptism, but in his words, "There was water. There was joy. So, in the sea, they baptized me."[13] Regrettably, this celebratory event brought about a sectarian clash of epic proportions.

Though he did not understand the severity of the problem, Turgay knew he was the cause of it. Father Luigi took him to the local monsignor, a higher authority in the Catholic Church, where the priests discussed his Protestant baptism and grumbled, "Turgay is our guy! They stole him!"[14] Later, the monsignor held a special mass for Turgay's confirmation in the Catholic Church, renaming him "Antoine" and reluctantly accepting his Protestant baptism.[15]

Meanwhile, during this period in the late 1970s through 1980, outside the walls of the church, political extremism was rampant and violent. "The authorities seemed unable to restore order," according to historian, Erik Zürcher.[16] Later events led to the third military intervention in Turkish politics in twenty years: "law and order problems, Kurdish separatism, a political system that seemed completely deadlocked and an economy in tatters. To this was added what seemed to many, both civilian and military, the threat of Islamic fundamentalism"[17] In one of our interviews, Turgay relayed that during this time, extremist groups on both sides of the political spectrum murdered some of his close friends, along with others he knew.[18]

Reflecting on that tumultuous period, Turgay noted that Jesus was his peace and safe harbor. He knew God personally. To have a relationship with God was a new and wonderful experience for him, especially because Islam's God is unknowable.

Still, he faced the same dilemma: the need to feel he belonged or was "at home" in the body of Christ. Both Protestants and Catholics claimed him as theirs. Because the Protestant brothers worshiped in Turkish (unlike the

13. Üçal, interview, July 8, 2013.

14. Üçal, interview, July 8, 2013.

15. Following this incident, St Antoine's Church changed the rules for new converts, requiring preparatory catechism classes and Catholic Communion. They forbade anyone else to baptize "their people."

16. Zürcher, *Turkey: A Modern History*, 276.

17. Zürcher, *Turkey: A Modern History*, 282.

18. This also was when the first modern-day Christian in Turkey lost his life (June 1979). David Goodman, a worker in Adana, was murdered by terrorists upon answering a knock at his front door.

Catholic priests, who used Latin in their masses) with chants closer in style to his Islamic background, Turgay decided to unite with them.

Suddenly, the Protestants divided. A huge internal dispute emerged, and there was a big blowup. Turgay remembers thinking, *If this is Christianity, I don't want to stay."* [19] Not knowing where to turn, Turgay eschewed any further engagement that year with Christians. He left the church.

After my interview, I could not forget this gloomy picture of Turgay's early experiences with evangelization. Later that evening, I took to my field notes to express the pent-up emotions:

> Parts of this first episode were really painful to hear. I hurt for "the young Turgay." Despite being amazed at God's unique way of leading him into the kingdom, I am ashamed of the contentious behavior of Turgay's Catholic and Protestant brothers. And of course, the unfamiliar vocabulary that the church leaders used in their sermons and spiritual conversations didn't make any sense to a Muslim seeker. Unfortunately, they didn't know about inculturation. I replayed parts of Turgay's lengthy narrative leading up to the resultant fractured relationships over and over in my mind, as I rode home in the *dolmuş* (minibus). I'm still feeling sick at heart over the alienation that occurred on more than one level for Turgay. He was by then a believer, looking for a community of fellow believers where he could feel at home. I wonder at times like these how Father continues to be patient and loving toward humankind.[20]

In our next interview session, Turgay picked up the thread of his story. He had no job and was not yet in college. Having just finished high school, he headed off to spend the summer with his grandparents in Mudanya. It was during this period of turmoil that Turgay found himself in crisis. This status quo would not change for another five years. In the fall, he rashly married a younger teenager, and shortly after that, his daughter was born. This combined with his pursuit of university studies while trying to make a living to support his young family kept him on edge. Was Turgay a true believer?

Turgay's conversion was a more complicated process than some people believe about the conversion narrative. Turgay had accepted Christ in 1979 at the age of seventeen, but his spiritual journey had twists and turns and was now in a place of seeming stagnation. In 1980, a military coup took place.

19. Üçal, interview, July 8, 2013.
20. Whittaker, field notes, 2013–2015.

There were fewer than a hundred Protestants in the country, and being a Turk automatically meant being a Muslim, so it was extremely dangerous or difficult to live as a disciple of Christ among Turkish citizens. Now looking back with remorse and self-reproach on his time with the Protestants, Turgay admitted, "I left the church, was confused, and then did a crazy marriage and started university. It was a terrible thing for my family, because I was so young. It was a mess, mess, mess! It was a big, big wrong!"[21]

His university classes were in the Arabic and Persian department of literature, meaning most classes were related to Islam. He also participated for a while in "the Light," the Nurcu Sufi religious movement. Still, as Turgay disclosed in our interview, in the midst of his circumstances, he met with Jesus. In the face of spiritual confusion, he looked for time to connect with God.

In 1984, Turgay was twenty-two, attending university, and moving into his new position at the famous Hachette international bookstore as director of the English-language department.[22] Turgay recognized that Jesus was his Savior and Lord and that he could not run away from Christ. But he did not know what to do about his lack of a spiritual community. He sometimes attended the Union Church of Istanbul, a nearby English-language, international Protestant church meeting in the Dutch consulate chapel. But it had a Western culture, and Turgay did not feel at home. What happened next is a marvelous testimony of God's power breaking into contemporary history.

DISCIPLESHIP IN COMMUNITY

As Turgay settled into his job, he began meeting the other employees at Hachette. Imagine his shock when he learned two young American colleagues were believers. They were staff members with a religious university organization called Campus Crusade for Christ (CCC).[23] A day or two later, Turgay met more Christian brothers. They worked next door in the

21. Üçal, interview, July 8, 2013.

22. Turgay's rare English-language proficiency as a Turk enabled his early employment: English school secretary for an Islamic college (two years) and education secretary for a political foundation of Prime Minister Turgut Özel (two years). Today, Hachette Livre is the fourth largest trade and educational book publisher in the world. Turgay considers each of these work experiences a blessing, because he learned a lot about dealing with people in a secular setting.

23. In 2011, the organization changed its name to Cru.

Bible Society bookshop.[24] So it was that God encircled Turgay with fellow believers in the workplace. Turgay began seeking out their company, and they soon became his spiritual community.

These Christian men had a great influence on Turgay. He met with the Bible Society friends at lunchtime every day and the CCC members outside of work for the next two years.[25] Miraculously, God provided a unique learning environment for developing Turgay's discipleship: a small group setting with the free exchange of viewpoints, the uncovering of his spiritual gifts, a ministry of healing, and the recognition of his leadership potential. With an emphasis on learning (Bible study, memorization of Scripture, and prayer), the practice became an ingrained joy and habit as Turgay matured in the Lord. Soon Turgay's concepts of the ultimate sacred concern took on greater scope and meaning.

Biblical and spiritual goals became clear as Turgay began applying them to real life. It was then that he began expressing his ideas and feelings to his friends for how he envisioned the possibility of a Turkish-led church. Thinking aloud, he would frequently muse, "I wish the Turkish church would be . . ." or "I wish the Turkish church could be . . ." and then fill in the blanks.

FIRST MINISTRY LEADERSHIP POSITIONS

In 1986, God gave Turgay the desire of his heart. He was unable to contain his excitement as he related to me this twenty-seven-year-old story:

> Someone told me that the Swedish consulate [next door to Hachette's] had a small chapel at the back of the property that was not being used, so I asked for permission to use it as a Christian meeting place. It didn't take long to get the okay. I worked at the bookstore, so they trusted me. My friends and I were ecstatic![26]

The strategically placed chapel provided a place to hold discipleship training for the converts coming to Christian faith through the ministry of Turgay and his CCC co-workers. It was a place where the courageous small band of believers could worship together on the Lord's Day. But what about a pastor for this nascent fellowship? They needed a Turkish pastor.

---

24. This was the same bookshop where Turgay had purchased his first Bible at age sixteen.

25. Üçal, interview, July 8, 2013.

26. Üçal, interview, July 8, 2013.

Thus, it was that in 1986, during the process of birthing a fellowship, the young congregation unanimously appointed Turgay as pastor of the Turkish Protestant Church (TPK in Turkish). This fellowship is now famously known as the first Turkish-led Protestant church community in Istanbul. Amazed at God's miraculous work in his life, Turgay commented,

> I never thought one day I would be a pastor! I never thought I would be a church planter! I was looking at myself and asking, "How will I live in my environment as a normal Turkish Christian, a very normal local believer of Christ?"[27]

Soon afterward, Turgay also joined the CCC staff, going through special organizational training and completing distance learning courses in Christian studies at Regent College in Vancouver, British Columbia, Canada.

Turgay and his teammates went on to evangelize and disciple multiple converts over the next five years. Many of today's national church leaders came to faith and were discipled in the church before embarking on their individual ministerial paths. One long-time worker claims that the total number exceeds twenty.[28]

Behind these joyful scenes, however, is a story of loss and grief. The demise of Turgay's rash teenage marriage occurred during this period. After a few years of marriage, he and his wife separated and later divorced. However, the trajectory of Turgay's life in Christian ministry became clear and total—God's plans are not thwarted. Later, the Lord brought Sibel, a devout Christian woman, into Turgay's life within the context of TPK. She was one of the many young people who flocked to the small chapel in the late 1980s to hear the eloquent young Turkish preacher. In time, she became one of the worship leaders. They married in 1992, the year he turned thirty.[29]

SEARCH FOR BELONGING

Meanwhile, Turgay's innovative mind was active. He began to ponder how to provide biblical education for the new converts, specifically through the lens of Turkish culture. He remembered telling workers, "We need

27. Üçal, interview, July 8, 2013.

28. D. H., interview, April 10, 2016.

29. Contentedly married for more than twenty-five years, Turgay and Sibel continue to minister together in worship each Sunday, honoring the balance between daily life, work, and care for family. (See Üçal family photo, along with other photos of Turgay and indoor/outdoor shots of a sample ASM Christmas outreach event in Appendix B).

education, education, education. I want a school, and how can we start a school? But it should be very Turkish, very local."[30] Today, this approach is characterized as *inculturation*.

As God would have it, Turgay's vision coincided with the 1989 arrival of retired Bible school teacher Mary Mitchell from Toronto, Canada. She had come to Istanbul to teach English at Marmara University, one of the oldest universities in Istanbul.

Describing how he met her in the kitchen of Canadian missionaries, Turgay's narration serves as documentation of the humble beginnings of *Bithynia* (now known as *Hasat*, an unofficial Christian education provider in Istanbul).[31] Mary's response to Turgay's vision surprised him:

> Mary said, "I'm a Bible school teacher, and I'd like to help you start a Bible school in Turkey. But I don't speak any Turkish. What can I do?"
>
> Turgay replied, "Forget about Turkish. Speaking Turkish is not important. What you do is more important. I'll be your mouth."[32]

In this way, the retired teacher and Turgay produced the courses and plans. Mary gave the lectures in English, and Turgay translated. Together, this unlikely pair founded the first Protestant training facility in Turkey, which is still equipping local believers, teachers, and church leaders today.

Some years later, Turgay left *Bithynia* to start a seminary on his own. While Mary insisted that all teachers be foreign, his vision was to find local qualified educators with Turkish accreditation so that the diplomas would be recognized in Turkey. In 2003, Turgay became the founder and academic dean of the Miami International Seminary's (MINTS) Turkish department, a distance-learning arm of the school located in Miami, Florida.[33] Operat-

---

30. Üçal, interview, July 8, 2013.

31. Organized as an association, *Hasat* (Harvest Church Ministries), works through seminars. It is not accredited, because no official theological education is permitted in Turkey outside of Islam.

32. Üçal, interview, July 8, 2013.

33. Miami International Seminary (MINTS) was founded in 2000 as a collaborative effort with church leaders and missionaries in Miami, Florida. While MINTS is not a denominational seminary and has members and students from a wide variety of backgrounds, it adheres to Reformed theology. The Westminster Confession of Faith serves as its main statement of faith. MINTS encourages a "school without walls" approach, where classes are held in churches, parks, home, and restaurants in the communities where people live. The school advocates taking the education to the people by having the professors go and establish new schools in an ever-expanding circle of communities rather than one central location. See http://mints.edu/ for more information.

ing out of the All Saints Moda (ASM) church office, it now has twenty-four graduates and 216 students who have taken courses.

Returning to the account of Turgay's losses in life, in addition to his first marriage, he also lost "the theology" of his church and ultimately the church itself, as a result of an American Vineyard pastor's visit to the tiny Christian community just before Turgay's compulsory military service. While Turgay was away for eight months, some of the recent converts Turgay had baptized were influenced toward the neo-charismatic movement. Upon his return, Turgay saw that many of the other believers also were influenced to move away from the Reformed faith tradition he and his CCC colleagues had originally established.[34] In response, Turgay resigned and left the church he had cofounded. It was a traumatic situation he was forced to accept.

In 1993, Turgay and Sibel started in their home an independent church: the Istanbul Presbyterian Church (IPC). By the end of the first year, it had outgrown their living room, so they moved the believers to an apartment fitted with carpet and benches for their "religious connection center:" a euphemism for a worship service they used in order to obtain governmental permission to meet as a Christian group. As Turgay's church ministry began to grow again, so did his profile as a Turkish Christian leader.

In 1996, CCC appointed him as its first Turkish national leader (a position in which he served for three years). At the same time, his growing congregation relocated to a larger permanent home: a vacant historic Anglican church built in 1878, All Saints Moda, where Turgay ceased using the acronym IPC. His church community, now called All Saints Moda (ASM), has been meeting in this building since All Saints Day, November 1, 1996. Its members are a mix of ethnicities, including Turkish, Armenian, Kurdish, Kazakh, Iranian, Russian, and Korean.

Through the years, international Christian periodicals[35] have taken an interest in Turgay's life story and ministry. His ministry opportunities have expanded to include defending the faith on radio and television, ministering in multiple foreign countries, and authoring sixteen books.[36] One Christian journalist has said that Turgay's personal story embodies the

---

34. Four of these men now serve as pastors or leaders in charismatic churches.

35. Carnes, "Jesus in Turkey," 25–28; and Wallace, "Devastation in Turkey," 1–4.

36. See Appendix A.

Part Two: Turgay Üçal, Agent of Change

"promise and peril" of Christianity in Turkey.[37] When did Turgay become a music maker—the embodiment of promise? What was the process?

MUSIC MAKER

At a high-profile 2002 interfaith *iftar*[38] dinner, Turgay suddenly stood up, surprising everyone. With a courteous nod to the guests who had previously introduced themselves, he commented, "If I may, I would also like to participate. May I sing this song?" Without hesitation, he began to sing his first composition:

> O all you nations, glorify the Lord
>
> O all you peoples, exalt him (refrain)
>
> Because his blessing is eternal
>
> Because his faithfulness is eternal
>
> Because his love is eternal.[39]

How appropriate for this gathering! As Huyser-Honig states, "You might think of Psalm 117 as ethnodoxology in a nutshell."[40]

Not recognizing that its text came from the Psalms, one Protestant couple in attendance thought the song was terrible because there was no Jesus in it. Conversely, there were believers from Turgay's church community who commented, "Wow, that's great! Let's sing it. Can we sing it at church?" So began Turgay's indigenous music-making ministry. Looking back on that evening, Turgay now understands that his song was the expression of his identity as an *İstanbuli*[41] follower of Christ. To him, it represented home and a sense of belonging.

Little did Turgay realize that the song heralded his future indigenous music making and was a harbinger of the musico-liturgical inculturation he soon introduced at ASM. His song was a sacred music form that Turkish society associates with religious people, a music form that belongs to them and performs an important function in their community. Encased in the Turkish

37. Carnes, "Jesus in Turkey," 25.

38. *İftar* is the evening meal with which Muslims end their daily Ramazan fast at sunset. It usually features an elaborate spread, especially if there are outside guests.

39. Üçal, Song 42 from Ps 117. The sacred lyrics of this category of songs is known as *glorification*.

40. Huyser-Honig, "Ethnodoxology: Calling all Peoples to Worship," line 86.

41. Turkish term for a resident of Istanbul.

traditional song form of the *şarkı*,[42] it presented a strong testimony of God, his transcendence, his immanence, and his love. It was easily recognizable as a devotional hymn of glorification—or doxology—across all three Abrahamic faiths. It sounded familiar to everyone in the room. However, with a distinctly oriental melody that was modal and chant-like, the music was far different from the music of Turkey's tiny Protestant community.

Today, questionable issues of identity and belonging for Muslim background believers (MBBs) in Turkey have emerged.[43] As the number of MBBs has increased and MBB congregations have come into existence worldwide, workers and Christian researchers, such as Charles Faroe, are raising questions about identity and a sense of belonging for MBBs in relation to applied theology. Faroe defines applied theology as forms of worship and how a church functions, including its leadership, congregational life, and practice.[44] He writes,

> Most if not all Muslim majority contexts are collectivistic, and conversion to Christianity by individuals or families tend to be quite disruptive. Hence, issues of identity and belonging are important for MBBs. Each Muslim context is different and MBBs' experiences should be considered locally.[45]

Coming into focus here is the literature on the MBB experience, and identity crisis appears to be a major refrain.[46] Belonging comes in at a distant second to identity, and perhaps is less frequently mentioned because scholars in various social disciplines, such as Nira Yuval-Davis, are inclined to envision identity as a part of belonging. She says,

> The politics of belonging involves not only constructions of boundaries, but also the inclusion or exclusion of particular people, social categories and groupings within these boundaries by those who have the power to do this. [47]

The terms inclusion and exclusion resonate with Turgay. He knows them firsthand. Since 2002, he has borne the brunt of the inclusionary and exclusionary boundaries in Turkey's Protestant church community

---

42. A Turkish art song form.

43. Zubaida, "Turkish Islam and National identity," 199.

44. Faroe, "Questioning Belonging," 1.

45. Faroe, "Questioning Belonging," 1.

46. Barnett, "Refusing to Choose," loc 861–866.

47. They exist, but they are not written down.

as they relate to his indigenous songs. Many Protestants in Turkey—both national Christians and workers—reject Turgay's songs for two reasons: (1) they consider it to be an identity marker of Islam, and/or (2) they have little or no appreciation for this indigenous song genre.[48] In contrast, many converts of national heritage in Turkey that embrace Turgay's hymnody do so, because they find identity and belonging in Christian songs that reflect their cultural heritage.

Turgay's attitude toward Western songs began to change in the late 1980s when he pastored his first church. Although he connected with some of the translated Western choruses, lyrics like the following seemed rare:

> I worship you; I worship you;
>
> The reason I live is to worship you.[49]

Songs filled with Western idioms and set phrases did not touch Turgay's heart. Believing that Turkish worship practice should not be a carbon copy of that of the West, he concluded he should use local music.

In response to the folk/pop song genre of the West's Evangelical Church in the 1970s and 1980s—so different from the music he knew and loved as a child—Turgay began composing better songs, or so he thought. He began to create songs in the Türk *Sanat Müziği* genre (Turkish *sanat* music, or TSM), using local metaphors and idioms.[50]

He does not expect everyone to understand his concept of musical inculturation, nor does he assume that the current Westernized Protestant churches will embrace it. He is coming from a different place: his own culture.[51]

Are not Turgay's worship songs helping to create the church, a spiritual home, for his assembly—a place where they can be their authentic selves without fear of judgment? The need for a sense of belonging in worship is universal.

48. Turgay claims that many MBBs in Turkey have had no connection with Islam. They say, "I was a Muslim," but he wonders how they mean that or describe that. They may have had a taste of it, but now ensconced in a Christian environment, they consider that it was a true Muslim background.

49. Perrin, "When I Look into Your Holiness," chorus.

50. This song form, known as *şarkı* (song), is the most well-known and universal urban art song form in Turkey (Bates, *Music in Turkey*, 41). Related to both urban and rural folk music, *şarkı* is described as a "national genre that encapsulates the emotional life of the Turks" by Klaser. In "From an Imagined Paradise to an Imagined Nation," 3.

51. Üçal, Interview, July 15, 2013.

Turgay's song texts are evocative of devotional texts from Turkey's synagogues, Orthodox Christian churches, and Islamic mosques, where glorification is the most important feature of worship and chanting is the rule. For the Jewish people, the central prayer is the Shema (Deut 6:4). Intoned three times daily by religious Jews, it encapsulates the monotheistic essence of their faith. For the Orthodox Church, the call to worship starts each day. Originating in the Office of Vespers, it is fundamental to the life and spirit of Orthodoxy, worshiping God, Father, Son, and Holy Spirit. For the devout Muslim, it is the Bismillah: "In the Name of God, most merciful and kind," a profound, humble expression used daily before undertaking any task or action and before the recitation of each chapter of the Qur'an, except for the ninth. Each in their unique way, these expressions of worship provided stimulus for Turgay's songs.

Worship is the chief focus of Turgay's life. It must not be entertainment; rather, it must be pure and untainted by secular leanings. He believes a foundation of prayer, the study of Scripture, and life in community are essentials for ongoing transformation. Is he a prophet or priest?

PROPHET AND PRIEST

In addition to characteristics of a musician, Turgay demonstrates the characteristics of both prophet and priest in his life and ministry. Even though the vast majority of the people in Turkey are Muslim, the country's geography and history hold an important place for Christianity. The role of the priest in the Eastern Orthodox and Catholic Churches is a part of the Turkish culture. Still, in the Protestant church, the preacher or church leader role is called pastor. In Figure 4, an adaptation of Hiebert, Shaw, and Tiénou's work,[52] I placed an asterisk before attributes I see as characteristic of Turgay. I also included my observations in italics. In some cases, I have marked both *prophet* and *priest* with an asterisk.

Turgay demonstrates both roles, displaying strengths in the church and educational institutions. Serving in a prophetic role beginning in 2000— "the year of religious tolerance" established by the government— Turgay was selected as the representative for the ecumenical community of Christian churches in Istanbul. This group includes the following denominations: Anglican, Armenian Apostolic, Catholic (Greek, Roman, Armenian, and Chaldean), Orthodox (Greek, Russian and Syriac), Assyrian Church of the East, and Protestant. For the next five years, he defended Christianity

52. Hiebert, Shaw and Tiénou, *Understanding Folk Religion*, 328.

in many dialogues with *imams* (Muslim spiritual leaders) on local TV talk shows and in newspapers. But after repeated warnings and threats of physical harm from different Muslim groups, he reluctantly withdrew from this high-profile position. It was too dangerous.

Turgay is secure in his divine call as pastor, teacher, and composer. His worship songs reveal his love of the Scriptures and his walk with God. They speak to the deeper facets of life.

In personality and behavior, Turgay is a charismatic figure, respected by people of all ages. Often invited to be the keynote speaker at local and international ministry events, he also leads worship for the participants, introducing his songs and chants. Both inside and outside the pulpit, Turgay displays the gregarious charismatic side of his personality through facial expressions and gestures. He enjoys a good laugh, especially with friends during extended meals together. Turgay and his family still live in the first apartment he and Sibel moved into as newlyweds in 1992. They live within their middle-class means.

Turgay's personality is typically calm and adept at working a programmed four-day office schedule at the church. He practices what he preaches and sings. The *spirituality defined* category was one that caught my attention, because Turgay holds to a wide range of spirituality. To listen to his prayers is to be led to the throne of God. There is a particular depth of feeling and meaning in his words, which points to a life lived in harmony with the sacred tradition of Scripture, liturgy, and prayer.

As to his training, he not only learned on the job in his first pastorate but also undertook formal theological studies that culminated in a doctorate. Turgay's education includes a BA in Arabic literature (Istanbul University), 1987; classes from Regent University in Canada, late 1980s and early 1990s; Master of Theological Studies (Chesapeake Reformed Theological Seminary), 2000; and a PhD in biblical theology from Miami International Seminary (MINTS) in southern Florida, 2007.[53]

SUMMARY

In this chapter, I explored Turgay's background. I discovered how he was surrounded by music in his early years. We can see how his pathway led to leadership early on. In middle adulthood, his music making burst into bloom and continues to grow. His life today reflects the dual roles of prophet

---

53. For a list of Turgay's publications and papers, see Appendix A.

and priest: Turgay unassumingly sustains the roles of prophet, priest (pastor), teacher (*hoca*) and composer/musician.

	PROPHETS	PRIESTS
FOUND	*When old structures are inadequate for new situations; times of social turbulence, political turmoil, and spiritual crisis *Sectarian conflict, divorce and remarriage, death threats and political turmoil*	*During times of relatve social stability and prosperity *Past 13 years*
APPOINTMENT	*Through inner certitude of a divine call to a particular task and human obedience *Assurance of a divine call*	Through the religious system; election training, installation, appointment, promotion *Representative for ecumentical churches; former leader of TEK (Turkish evangelical churches); Academic dean, Miami International Seminary: Turkish Department*
FOCUS	*On broad issues; idealistic, and a concern with past and future	*Proper procedures, rituals; realistic, concerned with the present
LEADERSHIP	*Charismatic	Bureacratic
LIFESTYLE	Frugal, simple, emphasizes communual living *Lives in community with those who share this value*	*Adapted to the community, preserves individual privacy
BEHAVIOR	*Emotionally expressive, eccentric	*Calm, temperate, programmed
ATTITUDE TO SIN	Intolerant, iconoclastic	*Allows for human failures and imperfections *Desires that sinners be restored*
COMMUNICATION WITH GOD	*Seeks direct access to God through personal revelation	*Seeks knowledge of God through public revelation
SPIRITUALITY DEFINED	*Inner piety and social involvement	*Living in harmony with sacred tradition *Holds to a wide range of spirituality*
NORMS	*God speaks to the specific time and situation	*Timeless laws and universal principles
AUTHORITY	*Personal charisma and spiritual	*Office and work *Requirements of a founding pastor*
ROLE AND FUNCTION	*Moral and ethical preacher, foreteller, exhorter of people to turn back to God	*Teacher of orthodox doctrine, guardian of tradition, minister at the altar in worship
TRAINING	*Apprenticeship on the job	Formal training prior to ministry
RELATION TO SOCIETY	Outside to judge and call to repentance	*Inside to maintain the religious culture
RELATION TO CHURCH	*Reformer, critic, detached, no territorial ties, no place in hierarchy *ASM is an independent Presbyterian church*	Guardian of tradition and creeds, tied to specific congregations, empowered, appointed and legitimatized by hierarchy
SELF-IDENTITY	*Outsider to other pastors in Turkey *As an innovator, he sometimes is perceived as someone outside the evangelical circle*	*Member of the religious organization (TEK)
CHANGE AGENT	*Social and spiritual reform, acts on existential truth, calls for dynamic changes	*Liturgical renewal, legislative reforms without schism, makes reforms at a moderate pace

Figure 4: Prophets and Priests

Excerpt from *Understanding Folk Religion* by Paul G. Hiebert, R. Daniel Shaw, and Tite Tiénou, copyright © 1999. Used by permission of Baker Academic, a division of Baker Publishing Group.

5

Worship at All Saints Moda

> Because Turgay became a practitioner of musico-liturgical in-
> culturation intuitively, I have had to analyze the meaning of
> what he has accomplished. Turgay does what comes to his mind
> in his desire to blend together the gospel message and his cul-
> ture. Metaphorically speaking, it is like planting flowers in the
> backyard to give it a homey feel. Flowers make it attractive to
> birds and people and give it that at-home atmosphere. Bevans
> and Schroeder talk about entering another person's garden as
> part of contextualization.[1] Roberta King has applied it in class
> as entering another person's musical garden. Turgay has moved
> beyond King's analogy: He is the tiller of the soil. He is working
> diligently in his cultural garden.[2]

IN CHAPTER 4, I described Pastor Turgay Üçal's background, his cultural
heritage, and his various roles in ministry, illustrating God's blueprint of
his early life. The purpose of chapter 5 is to explain the integrative way that
Turgay's inculturation of music and liturgy unfolds within an All Saints
Moda (ASM) worship event (summer 2012–spring 2015) by drawing from
the fields of ethnomusicology and ritual studies. The explanation is not
based on a single event; instead, it is based on the patterns and changes
that became apparent to me during my three years of fieldwork and was
indicated by conversation with Turgay and congregants.

1. Bevans and Schroeder, *Constants in Context*, loc. 1438.
2. Whittaker, field notes, 2013–2015.

Ethnomusicologists Alan Merriam,[3] Gerald Béhague,[4] and Regula Qureshi[5] have emphasized the importance of an integrated study of music within its context. Every dimension must be understood and addressed as inherently linked.

I adopted an event-centered analysis from ethnomusicology as appropriate for interpreting ASM's musico-liturgical ritual practice. An event-centered analysis is simply that—it focuses on the event, both the music making itself and music as a type of action within the ritual event. Everything that happens within this context, including the exchanges between the participants, is essential to the analysis of music making. This interpretive framework is a device to elicit full descriptions and not mere summaries of the values and beliefs implicit in the field of ritual. The goal is to trigger insight into the worship event. I was an active participant in this analysis.

In addition to exploring ASM's ritual practice, I also applied Ronald Grimes's methodology of mapping the field of ritual.[6] This involves six interactive elements: (1) ritual time (2) ritual space (3) ritual objects (4) sound and language (5) ritual identity, and (6) ritual action. Following the liturgical sequence of worship, I demonstrate these vital ritual elements via table form.

LITURGY

Though liturgy may be understood narrowly as complicated elaborate rituals, there is a broader meaning in the printed pages or the authorized rituals handed down through the centuries. My focus was on the performed liturgy as well as the lived-out liturgy that merges the lives of ASM believers with the worship of God. Turgay has substantially revised the content since the church's founding, borrowing from other traditions.

The three Abrahamic faiths originated in the same region—the Middle East—and are uniquely linked to one another. Thus, parts of the ASM liturgical practice overlap those of the Jewish, Orthodox Christian, and Islamic faiths, intersecting in the cultural borderlands and border crossings. See Figure 5. Though there are sharp differences and disputes among them, there are common religious practices. With a built-in appreciation for his cultural heritage, Turgay views Islam as an ally. Since the pillars of Islam

3. Merriam, *Anthropology of Music*, 32.

4. Béhague, *Performance Practice*, 7–9.

5. Qureshi, *Sufi Music of Indian and Pakistan*, 57.

6. Grimes, *Beginnings in Ritual Studies*, 19–32.

are adaptations of earlier Jewish and Christian forms, he views it as reusing what originally belonged to these faith communities.

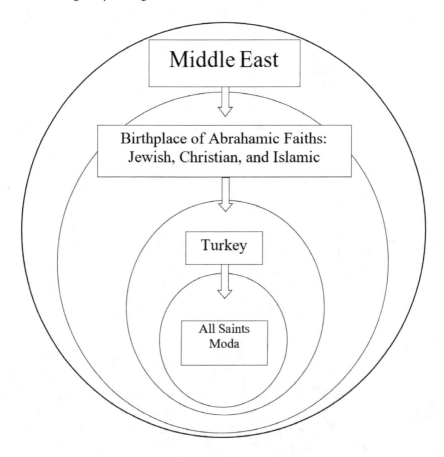

Figure 5: Influences on ASM Worship Praxis

SUNDAY WORSHIP EVENT

Every Sunday, approximately sixty to a hundred people—primarily adults[7]—attend the 11:00 a.m. worship service at ASM. The highlight of the week for

7. Parents with Western ideals regarding the spiritual training of children take their youngsters to the next-door church office suite during the worship service. Here, a team of moms jointly lead Sunday school lessons, activities, and crafts for the kids, although Turgay prefers that children remain with their parents in the sanctuary, as it is more culturally appropriate in a Middle Eastern setting.

many in the community, this liturgical event is the primary time for followers of Christ to gather and experience the shared faith that sustains them during life's daily challenges. The service usually lasts an hour and a half, with some making time before and after the liturgy for fellowship, either in the church or on the grounds of the church. Occasionally, the community celebrates events in the life of the church with food after the service.

Liturgy, word, and song make up the oral culture tradition of this assembly. Many worshipers recite the ritual and sing the songs from memory, with visitors and a few others following along in the Daily Worship prayer book (*Vakit İbadeti*).[8] The familiar liturgy and music cultivate a meaningful worship service, with congregants standing or gently swaying during particular periods of singing. Assembly members know that God will be present and the Holy Spirit will move in their midst.

A key worship tool (alongside the Bible), ASM's custom-designed prayer book is similar to a *siddur*, the Jewish prayer book, which also contains a set order of daily prayers. In contrast, while there are Muslim devotional books by individuals associated with a Sufi order, these are not readily available to the public.

What is unique about the ASM prayer book? An intricate-patterned Gallic cross of a geometric design is on the cover. Scattered throughout the inside are colorful depictions of Ottoman artwork, both geometric and floral, along with various objects. The tulip, a symbol of Istanbul (introduced to Anatolia in the eleventh century by the Seljuk Turks), is a reoccurring detail. The three-petal visual pattern is well suited and well placed for amplifying Turgay's emphasis on the Trinity. See ASM prayer book cover with sample Ottoman artwork in Appendix F.

There are no human images in the ASM prayer book. The decision not to include them was strategic on Turgay's part. Turgay knows that many Muslims think images of the human form are idolatry, which is forbidden in the Qur'an. He also understands the importance of an artistic presentation of Islamic holy books, so the familiar appearance was intentional. Mary McGann, like Turgay, sees prayer books as essential worship tools, since "they formulate perspectives, procedures, and patterns that shape local performance, and situate a particular community's worship within a larger sphere of practice."[9] They function symbolically as part of the meaning making in ASM's worship.

8. Üçal, *Vakit İbadeti*, 2013–2015.

9. McGann, *Exploring Music as Worship and Theology*, 16.

ASM has a fixed liturgy. In fixed liturgy, one knows what is going on. The words have sunk in from the repetition from month to month and year to year. A liturgical worship approach aids in meditation and prayerful reflection.[10]

A few singular events, such as baptisms or baby dedications, occur on a requisite basis. Sunday liturgy expands as needed to accommodate important church family occasions.

The typical sequence of worship elements in ASM's liturgy are listed in Table 4. They point to a favorable comparison of participant involvement (A) when contrasted with non-liturgical churches. Music-related elements (B), occurrences of indigenous chant (C), and piano-accompanied musical elements (D) fill in the other elements of the liturgy.

Framework of the Liturgical Action

Sometime before the informal gathering, Turgay walks slowly through the church, gently swinging a censor of coals burning frankincense (see Table 4, #1). The ritual is part of the preparation for worship. The fragrance fills the room and then slowly dissipates, leaving an amazing lingering scent. It represents the mystery of God and his presence among the people.[11]

---

10. A "fixed" liturgy does not mean that every ASM worship event is exactly alike. Actually, no two Sunday worship events are. Turgay, ever sensitive to the leading of the Holy Spirit, may pause at any time, requesting people sit or stand, participate in meditative prayer or corporate prayer aloud, or spontaneously sing a song. The congregation normally stands for the five programmed songs and all liturgical prayers.

11. Frankincense was one of the herbs used to make the incense in the temple (Exod 30:34–38).

Table 4: Order of the Sunday Liturgy—All Saints Moda

	Elements of Worship	A	B	C	D
1	A censor is used to spread the aroma of incense throughout the church	Turgay			
2	Informal gathering				
3	No prelude—the short Westminster clock-chime melodic motive followed by eleven strokes on the hour begin the liturgy				
4	Liturgical Call to Worship—prayer (indigenous chant)	Turgay/All	I	C	
5	Exaltation—one or two Psalms—prayer (indigenous solo chant)	Turgay	V	C	
6	First song (Turkish translated Western song)	All	V	S	X
7	Second song (Turkish translated Western song)	All	V	S	X
8	Third song (Turkish translated Western song)	All	V	S	X
9	Exaltation (the congregation is encouraged to offer prayers and Scripture readings of praise)	All	I		
10	Offering (with both familiar and introduction of new Turgay songs)	Deacons take up offering (Music: Sibel/pianist)	V	S	X
11	Offertory Prayer	Deacon			
12	The Way of Meaning—study in the Scriptures (sermon)	Turgay			
13	Fourth song (indigenous responsive chant)	All	V	S	X
14	Transition song to "bow downs" (indigenous)	All	I	S	
15	Brief introductory prayer (indigenous solo chant)	Turgay	I	C	
16	Exaltation (indigenous responsive chant)	Turgay/All	I	C	
17	Brief introductory prayer (indigenous solo chant)	Turgay	I	C	
18	The Lord's Prayer (spoken or sung as an indigenous song)	All	I	Varies	
19	Brief introductory prayer (indigenous solo chant)	Turgay	I	C	
20	The Amida Prayer (adaptation of the eighteen-blessing Jewish prayer) (indigenous chant)	All	I	C	
21	Improvised indigenous song	All	V	S	
22	Scripture passage—according to the day of the month in the prayer book	Appointed Reader			
23	A creed Turgay created by blending two third century creeds (spoken)	All			
24	Confession of Faith—I Timothy 16:3 (spoken)	All			
25	Passing the Peace (Background music: Jewish tune with "Peace Be Unto You" lyrics)	All	I	S	X
26	Brief introductory prayer	Church Leader	I	C	
27	Communion prayer	Church Leader			
28	Breaking of bread—pouring of serving cups	Church Leader			
29	Scripture reading (responsive)	Church Leader/All			
30	Serving of Communion at the altar (dip bread into wine cup) Believers form a line down the middle aisle of the church (with both familiar songs and introduction to new Turgay songs)	Church Leader/All (Music, Sibel/pianist)	V	S	X
31	Announcements	Turgay			
32	Closing song (indigenous)	All	V	S	X
33	Pastoral blessing and dismissal	Turgay			
34	Postlude: reprise of Jewish folksong tune with "Peace Be Unto You" lyrics	(Music: Sibel/pianist)	I	S	X
35	Informal fellowship	All			

91

Key:

Column A: leaders or participants

Column B: elements performed musically:

V=variable selection I=invariable selection

Column C: distinction of elements performed musically:

C=chant S=song

Column D: piano accompaniment

The opening of the liturgy unfolds smoothly, progressing from relaxed fellowship (Table 4, #2) to a formal beginning in a quick and musical approach. The service begins with the recorded sound of Westminster's famous chime melody and eleven strokes on the hour (Table 4, #3).[12] Conversations hush and gradually fade into silence. Pastor Turgay rises from the front pew, takes three small steps to the center of the altar rail, and stops, facing the same direction as the assembly. The people rise to their feet. His action symbolizes a withdrawal from the profane world and a stepping forward to approach the divine presence of God. After the call to worship, Turgay takes three steps back, mirroring the three forward steps taken at the beginning. He explained that he steps back in the same way a subject would take leave of his king. In this instance, it is the King of kings and Lord of lords.[13] Turgay's forward and backward steps are modeled after the Jewish prayer ritual, although Turgay's actions are slightly different.[14] Both the call to worship and the prayer of glorification after the sermon preserve this symbolic approach.

The last Westminster chime is still echoing when Turgay lifts his head and with raised arms loudly proclaims the holiness of God. The first phrase of the call to worship is "Most Holy, Most Holy, Most Holy, Lord God Almighty" (Table 4, #4). This symbolizes opening the door to the mystery of God. The sound increases in volume and the energy rises, as with one voice the people join Turgay in the glorification of the Lord, chanting, "Heaven and earth give glory and praises to thee / All glory, all glory, all glory to the Name." The refrain is chanted a second time, beginning with "Hallelujah,

---

12. The Westminster chimes are very English, but since the British built the Anglican edifice during the Crimean War, it makes sense. Turkey maintains this aural tradition as a part of the history of the church.

13. Üçal, interview, September 1, 2013.

14. Donin, *To Pray as a Jew*, loc. 1447.

hallelujah, hallelujah, Lord God Almighty." This powerful occurrence introduces the communal and liturgical focus.

The call to worship is chanted, signaling inculturation. The text reinforces the observation. The final phrase of the opening chant is "Glory and honor [repeated three times] to the Name." I wondered why Turgay did not say "to Thee," "to your Name," or "to thy Name," until I read Constance Padwick's book, *Muslim Devotions,* and learned that the "Name" term is drawn from Ps 20:7: "But we will make mention of 'the Name of the Lord our God.'"[15] The qur'anic use of the term is like the Hebrew, making mention of "the Name of the Lord."[16] Used in invocation and worship, it addresses "the Name."[17] Turgay explained, "I begin the service like this, because this is our custom when we are starting something."[18] Just as Jewish services have the Bar'chu and Islam services have the Adhan, ASM has a call to worship that speaks to the spiritual expectations and cultural needs of its assembly.

A two-part form of Calvin's seventeenth-century Reformed understanding of communal worship characterizes the liturgical frame of ASM. The first part focuses on the Word—prayer, scriptural chanting/readings, songs and preaching (see Table 4, #4–12), followed by prayers and the Lord's Table (Table 4, #15–30). With a contemporary feel provided by translated Western ballads, the first part of the liturgy continues to the end of Turgay's sermon, the transitional point. Turgay explained the placement of the next several liturgical elements of the service:

> Before going to the Lord's Supper, I draw from the traditional Jewish synagogue tradition [Table 4, #12–20], taking twenty-first-century believers figuratively to the first-century Jesus in the synagogue. It means they should seek spiritual cleansing before I take them to the Lord's Table. We go to Gethsemane together through glorification and the *Amidah*, the eighteen-blessing prayer, an effective worship tool. Jesus comes in the congregation of Israel and then takes us with them and dies in front of Israel for salvation. Then after the cross and resurrection, the believers will be with him.[19]

Turgay asserts that the goal is the level of the image of God, and when one receives the Lord Jesus Christ, that level becomes complete.

15. Padwick, *Muslim Devotions,* 13.
16. Padwick, *Muslim Devotions,* 15, 87.
17. Padwick, *Muslim Devotions,* 14.
18. Üçal, interview, September 1, 2013.
19. Üçal, interview, September 1, 2013.

Part Two: Turgay Üçal, Agent of Change

The level represents wholeness, completeness, or readiness for the Lord's Table. But first comes the exchange of the peace (Table 4, #25), a period of animated greetings that includes the phrase "Peace be with you," often accompanied by the Turkish cultural double-cheek kissing gesture offered in Christian friendship and love.

While people greet one another, the musicians heighten the activity with lyrics that repeat the refrain "Peace be with you / peace be with you" set to a lively anonymous Jewish melody. These friendly interactions last about two minutes. When the music stops, a transition not unlike the beginning of the liturgy takes place. The informal exchanges lead to focused concentration and silence.

The Sunday worship event spans an hour and a half, including the announcements before the benediction (Table 4, #31). During this time, Turgay welcomes visitors and invites them to introduce themselves. On any Sunday, visitors may encompass local people, American church groups, or church leaders from various foreign countries. Frequently, a visitor may say he or she has felt the presence of God in the service. These words of encouragement are well received by the community. Announcements may include community events, invitations to attend special services, weddings, or concerts. All this is part of the leave-taking or goodbyes beyond the liturgy (Table 4, #31–35).

Each Sunday's worship event reminds the people of various interactive cycles of the assembly's life, including liturgical, sacramental, familial, and personal. ASM celebrates five liturgical seasons: Advent, Christmas, Lent, Easter, and Ordinary Time. Correspondingly, the liturgical colors at ASM are blue, red, lavender, gold, and green. These appear as coverings on the windows, the pulpit, and the Lord's Table. The Easter and Christmas celebrations are special occasions with festive foods, as is November 1, All Saints Day, and also the anniversary of the IPK's move to the ASM campus in 1996.[20] Family celebrations include weddings and child dedications. Music making—both singing and instrumental accompaniment—is a vibrant and permeating feature of each of these events. Ash Wednesday is the only somber observance in the church year. Where does the worship event occur?

20. The name, Istanbul Presbyterian Church, was changed to All Saints Moda upon the congregation's move to the ASM campus.

THE ROOM

One enters the church through two sets of double doors at the entrance to the worship space (see Figure 6). It is a large room and furnished in a manner fitting for an Anglican church built in England during the 1870s.[21] The room offers three open spaces that are likely spaces for movement and action. Two greeters, Jaklin and Ani[22] stand inside the entrance to the gathering area (A) to offer smiles and handshakes (or prayer books, if needed)[23] to those arriving for the service.

The center aisle (B) runs from the entry through the narthex and nave (main assembly area) to the front of the oblong room. It is the place for movement through the church in addition to being a likely meeting place for participants during the exchange of the peace. The aisle separates the eleven rows of padded benches on either side (C) through roughly two-thirds of the room. The focal point of activity is in the front of the building (D–K).

21. There is no lavatory in this historic building. Fortunately, the church office is just next door.

22. They are deaconesses and Turgay's assistants in the church office.

23. Many assembly members have memorized the liturgy or bring their own prayer books.

Figure 6: Moda Church: The Room

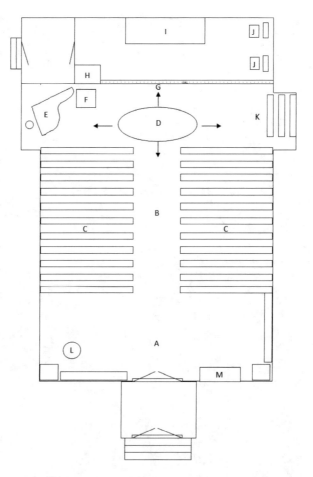

A. Gathering area   H. Pulpit

B. Center aisle   I. Communion table

C. Pews   J. Seating for Turgay and pastoral assistant

D. Open space   K. Seating for male church leaders

E. Grand piano   L. Baptismal font

F. Worship leader   M. Sand-filled candleholde

G. Altar rail

Pastor Turgay prefers to position himself in the open space between the altar and pews (D), a position central to the gathering. From there, he constantly moves in every direction, down the aisle through roughly two-thirds of the room. Other actions occur in the same location.

A baby grand piano (E) and pianist sit directly opposite in the west side of the cruciform. The worship leader (Sibel, wife of Turgay) stands nearby (F). After standing in line down the single aisle, the bread and wine are distributed to believers while they kneel at the altar rail (G) that runs across the front portion of the room. The platform contains various church furnishings. The pulpit (H) is never used during worship. However, the wooden communion table (I) on the one-step level platform is the centerpiece of the worship environment. It is used each Sunday during communion, as the sacrament's ritual objects (silver chalices, matching plates, and a pitcher) are kept on the table.

Sometimes the presider (typically Turgay) and his assistant may sit on the platform (J). Other church leaders who help to serve this open communion tend to sit in the east side of the cruciform (K). A baptismal font (L) and sand-filled candleholder (M) are located just inside the entrance, the font on the left and candles on the right. Running across the front and along the sides of the room are eleven colorful stained-glass windows that depict Bible scenes and stories. On sunny days, the windows create a radiance that fills the room. The room's steep vaulted ceiling with its custom-sized wooden beams extends the height of the room.

Acoustically speaking, the church is a good-sounding room. A single voice is heard without amplification throughout the worship space. However, Sibel uses a standing microphone. It boosts the volume of her lead voice, making it distinguishable during congregational singing.

To actively nurture a warm and friendly environment, the area in front of the altar is simple. For the same reason, All Saints Moda does not use a projector, screen, large speakers, electric keyboard, or guitars. The aesthetic effect for the first-time visitor is peace and serene beauty. This setting is welcoming to Orthodox Christians and Muslim background believer (MBB) visitors alike, since the worship environments are similar.[24]

The liturgical framework of ASM provides a good introduction to the various musical facets in the assembly's worship. For instance, a

---

24. Christians in Turkey are not allowed to construct new church building. Most Protestant fellowships worship together in storefronts, flats, or house churches. Reuse of historic churches like ASM is rare.

combination of nineteen episodes of song or chant occurs during each liturgy (see Table 6, column C). Three of these are communal liturgical chants used invariably: the call to worship (4), responsive exaltation (16), and the Amidah Prayer (20), in addition to three songs used invariably (14, 25, 34). Eight other song episodes (6–8, 10, 13, 21, 30, 32) are used variably. To this Turgay adds solo cantillations of one or two variable psalms, immediately following the call to prayer (5) and three brief introductory invariable prayers to different segments of the liturgy (15, 17, 26). The pianist accompanies congregational singing during the five scheduled songs and plays during the offertory, exchange of peace, communion, and postlude (6–8, 13, 32, 10, 25, 30, and 34).

Congregational music making is a vibrant practice of the ASM community, although musical leadership is essential to what takes place. Musicking is a means to a divine encounter.

Embodiment of liturgy and acoustic sound expressions—verbal exclamations, rhythmic clapping, and applause—are ways of contributing to the song event during the worship. Making a joyful noise to the Lord with praise, thanksgiving, and supplication is a given among assembly members.

Who leads worship at ASM? Titon writes, "How the community relates to the music makers also has a profound effect on the music."[25] This is in keeping with the communication theory that associates the communicator with the message itself. Donald Smith writes, "The communicator is the container, and the container inevitably shapes the message."[26] The church leadership team provides musical leadership at ASM, with Turgay as the main worship leader.

Because the musical leadership team is also the church leadership team (the medium), the potential impact of the music (the message) on the assembly is strengthened. This aspect is a plus. The leadership effectiveness of Turgay and other strong musical leaders reinforces the transformational effect of hymnody on the entire church assembly.

The church pianist arrived at All Saints Moda in 2000. She is a classically trained Russian musician, with significant skills that unify the musical team. Her improvisations provide inspiring accompaniments for congregational participation. The pianist is married to Reşit (*bendir*[27] player and unofficial associate pastor), and the couple's thirteen-year-old

---

25. Titon, *Worlds of Music*, 18.

26. Smith, *Creating Understanding*, 105.

27. A large frame Turkish hand drum.

daughter—a budding violin prodigy—frequently plays offertories and accompanies congregational song. Turgay leads the worship event, along with his wife, Sibel, the lead singer.

The *şarkı* is melodically and rhythmically produced—piano and *bendir* accompaniment provide the melodic and rhythmic support for its musical style. A *kanun* (zither-like instrument) and oud (lute) would be more culturally appropriate, but the assembly currently has no such instrumentalists. There is no church choir. Currently, there is no one in the congregation to lead it.

The assembly's musical practice involves a ten-week rotating schedule of fixed repertoire used throughout the year. It incorporates a blend of Turgay's indigenous works with locally translated choruses from around the globe, generally ballad style (see appendix G). It does not accommodate an influx of Western songs or choruses (the praise band model in contemporary Christian music embraced by many Protestant churches in Turkey). Comparing the pop style worship music Western churches use to the worship practice of ASM, Turgay believes "a pop style would detract from what we're here for."[28] He's convinced that the style does not suit the cultural sensitivities of his congregation and contemplative Eastern worship. ASM's worship practice accommodates the untrained singer—it avoids wide melody ranges, overlong note lengths, and overly syncopated rhythms. These fine points help us to understand Turgay's philosophy of worship music.

All worship team members have input into the song selection, but Turgay makes the final call. He has established criteria for whether a song is suitable to use in worship. McGann, writing about the topic, holds to the same stance: "Choices about . . . repertoire, decisions about why particular patterns of musical performance are maintained or altered, are related to the dynamics of leadership and musical authority within the community."[29]

Because Turgay is building a repertoire—a corpus of music he will draw from again and again—he shuns church music that lacks quality and relevance for authentic worship. Instead, he looks for songs that fit the liturgy, are biblically based and theologically sound, and have good musical quality, lyrically and melodically.

It should be noted that the ten-week song schedule lists three translated Western and just two of Turgay's songs each week. This is deceiving, for Turgay mixes in his indigenous songs a cappella throughout the

---

28. Üçal, interview, September 22, 2013.

29. McGann, *Exploring Music as Worship and Theology*, 23.

service. "My concern is that the Turkish ethnic character must not be lost," Turgay remarks in justifying the wide usage of his music in the worship event.[30] Observing that MBBs and former Orthodox Christians are accustomed to predictability in worship—a matter related to culture—Turgay contends that it is all the more reason for musico-liturgical inculturation in Turkey. What about ritual action? How might Muslim background seekers or converts and former Orthodox Christians receive inculturation of that aspect of worship?

Movement and gesture are important elements in the ASM liturgy, for with our body worship, we express the attitude of our hearts. Theologian James Fowler writes, "With liturgy we deal with the *kinesthetics* [the sensory experience] of faith. Through the teaching power of sacrament and worship, faith gets into our bodies and bone marrow."[31] An action or gesture can carry significant spiritual meaning. Westerhoff argues that "the rituals and ceremonials of a person's primary community is the most important influence in the shaping of faith, character, and consciousness."[32] Often, too, performing many of these acts of body worship collectively helps worshipers to identify with others, strengthening a sense of unity.

Chanted prayers at ASM have added postures: standing and bowing. In terms of uplifted hands, some hold their hands chest high with palms facing upward (also a Muslim prayer position) and others hold arms outstretched or straight up.

Bowing

Bowing during prayers conveys an attitude of humility, reverence, and worship. This customary motion in ASM worship events consists of the belt-low bow, the most widespread type of bow. The assembly bows in two chanted prayers, for a total of seven times:[33]

- The congregation bows three times during the glorification prayer (at "Hallelujah, Justifier, Sanctifier, and Glorifier") on the first word of each congregational response.

---

30. Üçal, interview, November 20, 2013.

31. Fowler, "Weaving the New Creation," 181.

32. Westerhoff, "Liturgy and Catechetics," 514.

33. Levias, "Numbers and Numerals," article 11619. The number seven is "the most sacred number" of Judaism, the general symbol for all association with God, because number one cannot be counted; seven also is a very important word for completion.

- The congregation bows four times during the *Amidah* Prayer (at "O Lord of the Universe," in the beginning of each section).

In addition to these bowing actions incorporated into the liturgy, there are other customary motions. Gestures are a performed part of each worship event.

GESTURES

Grimes defines a gesture in the broad sense as a synonym for attitude. He explains, "An attitude is not simply a state of mind or set of values; it is the total bearing of a body expressing a valued style of living."[34] Common gestures to chanting and music at ASM occur during the *Amidah* Prayer and the exchange of the peace. The first is an invariable gesture, and the second is variable.

Near the end of the *Amidah* Prayer, worshipers turn their heads to the right and chant, "Grant us a life that is *Christlike*." They then turn their heads to the left and chant, "And *Spirit-filled*." Facing forward again, they conclude with the words "And may our days be long until you take us in death into your presence."[35]

During the exchange of the peace, worshipers typically initiate a greeting by shaking hands. They are to seek peace with each other before seeking peace with God. Those with mutual affection for one another may embrace or kiss each other on both cheeks, Turkish style, as mentioned earlier. Gestures in worship are a form of inculturation.

Inculturation can be challenging. Turgay has changed the meaning of some traditional forms to fit ASM's culture, but others he has not, because they are too closely connected to Muslim religious beliefs. In the case of movements, gestures, and music, however, the forms can be used to express Christian meaning, because they are not specifically connected

34. Grimes, *Beginnings in Ritual Studies*, 57.

35. *Amidah* gestures are appropriated from those in the last step of the Muslim prayer ritual, when worshipers carry out the following instructions: "Turn your head to the right and say, '*As Salam Alaykum was Rahmatullahi wa Barakatuh.*' The angel who records your good deeds is to this side. Turn your head to the left and say, '*As Salam Alaykum was Rahmatullahi wa Barakatuh.*' The angel who records your wrongful deeds is to this side." Muslims must greet the two angels—supposedly sitting on each shoulder that keep track of their good and bad deeds—in this way before terminating the prayer ritual ("Performing the Muslim Prayers"; Part 2, 9. https://www.wikihow.com/Pray-in-Islam#:~:text=%20Performing%20the%20Muslim%20Prayers%20%201%20Make,your%20chest%2C%20or%20between%20the%20two%3B%20More%20).

to non-Christian meanings and because they have the potential to effectively convey the intended meanings. How does inculturation interact with ASM's liturgical theology?

LITURGICAL THEOLOGY

Like liturgical theologians Aidan Kavanagh,[36] Jill Crainshaw, and Gordon Lathrop, Turgay holds to the basic distinction of two theological categories as important to liturgical theology. He understands primary liturgical theology as "the communal meaning of the liturgy exercised by the gathering itself,"[37] expressed through the church's use of words and symbols to speak of God. It calls for participation to grasp the meaning. Secondary liturgical theology, on the other hand, is "written and spoken discourse that attempts to find words for the experience of the liturgy and illuminate its structures, intending to aid a more profound experience for congregants."[38] As a written discipline, it contributes to the depth of reflections that emerge from the interactions of the people.

In the context of the wisdom of Judeo-Christian tradition, Turgay's liturgical theology has a faith journey of praxis to theory to praxis—from communal tradition or actions to critical reflection on those actions to renewed communal action.

> The goal of this journey is to enable a faith community to experience life with a new understanding of what is ultimate . . . as the assembly encounters God in authentic liturgy, participants are enabled to look at the world and their existence in a new way.[39]

From this perspective, participants can be identified as having spiritually grown. This perspective within the liturgical movement connects with inculturation, for "the reflection of many on the worship of different churches in the world is that that there is something inadequate at the cultural level," according to Phillip Tovey.[40] He continues,

> It is this reflection on liturgical praxis/experience that has led to this particular conclusion, and reflection on the assembly in its cultural context is giving rise to new inculturated liturgies . . . The

36. Kavanagh, *On Liturgical Theology*, 7–8.
37. Lathrop, *Holy Things: A Liturgical Theology,* loc. 116.
38. Lathrop, *Holy Things: A Liturgical Theology,* loc 139.
39. Crainshaw, *Wise and Discerning Hearts*, 251.
40. Tovey, *Inculturation of Christian Worship*, 152–53.

aim is transformative. The method is that of reflection experience to lead to critical action.[41]

In my study of Turgay's worship music as outlined in this chapter, I have discovered that the outcome of his years of reflection on the ASM liturgy in its local context has resulted in today's musico-liturgical inculturation. Having reached his transformative goals for the liturgy, Turgay's critical action has led to the transformation of the assembly. What is the result of Turgay's experience with praxis—theory—praxis in theology?

CONTEXTUAL THEOLOGY

In view of local culture, Christian tradition (translation, anthropological, and praxis), and the biblical witness, Turgay's approach to the kingdom of God most closely mirrors Stephen Bevans's synthetic model of contextual theology.[42] This honors the traditional message while accepting the importance of taking all the facets of context seriously. Bevans underlines the strongest facet of this model: "its basic methodological attitude of openness and dialogue."[43] He is clear, even eloquent about this: "In our contemporary postmodern world so filled with . . . plurality and ambiguity, truth will not be reached by one point of view trying to convince all the others that it alone is correct" (93). Similarly, dialogue is at the heart of Turgay's concept of witness. To put his approach in perspective, Turkey is a country where Islam is prominent, where 67 percent of the Muslim population say religion is very important to them.[44] What is the result of Turgay's experience with praxis—theory—praxis in the sermon paradigm?

SERMON PARADIGM

Turgay's priority is teaching his people basic biblical concepts. His approach is to teach or preach in the oral culture tradition of Turkey (biblical mode of stories, illustrations, and cultural metaphors), enhancing the explanation of a passage's importance and how it applies to everyday life. He follows the example of Jesus, who used illustrations from nature and human life in the Synoptic Gospels. See Table 5 for an illustration of Turgay's approach to the parable of the sower in Matt 13.

41. Tovey, *Inculturation of Christian Worship*, 152–53.
42. Bevans, *Models of Contextual Theology*, 88–102.
43. Bevans, *Models of Contextual Theology*, 93.
44. Lynch, "How Muslims really think about Islam," *Foreign Policy* podcast.

Table 5: Parable of the Sower—Levels of Response to the Gospel [45]

Levels		Characteristics	Attitude
Inanimate	Rock	Spiritually dead, will never "get it"	Most people are in the inanimate level because they don't have any interest in spirituality.
Vegative	Plant	"Gets it" for a while, but then walks away	Has some interest. Comes to church occasionally at Christmas or drops in at other times of the year.
Animate	Animal	"Thinks" of him/herself as a believer in some way, but attends church mostly for personal gain (taking).	Wants to go to heaven, but never shares Christ with others.
Messianic	Human	Christlike in character, displaying the fruits of the spirit (giving).	Is a mature believer, sharing Christ with others and giving of his/her resources

Turgay uses concrete examples of a rock, plant, animal, and human to specify the four responses described in Matt 13. An inanimate rock represents the person who dies because Satan draws him or her away. A plant, signifying the vegetative level, illustrates someone who starts well but folds under pressure. The animal, or animate-level person, is one who gets sidetracked. This person wants to go to heaven but is too busy to share the faith or give of his or her resources. This person is a taker. Conversely, the human, or Messianic-level individual, understands the Word, matures into Christlikeness, and reflects the fruits of the Spirit. This person lives to worship and serve, share the faith, and give to those in need.

Through sermons that offer scriptural study enhanced by face-to-face dialogue and discussion, Turgay is discipling believers in ministry and witness. Assembly members bring friends to the services; others find their way to All Saints Moda through related circles. Conversions typically follow the web pattern along family, friendship, and occupational lines, resulting in baptisms[46] of new converts at ASM approximately three times a year.

45. Üçal, interview, September 1, 2013. Notice Turgay's use of the parable form for explaining a spiritual concept in his oral culture. This is an example of his teaching approach in sermons and personal discussions of spiritual concepts.

46. Turgay typically baptizes converts by affusion (pouring). He believes in total emersion; he baptized one of his three daughters in the sea. However, ASM, like Turkey's other historic church buildings constructed in the nineteenth century, lacks a baptistery.

MAPPING THE FIELD OF RITUAL

The preceding information was a full description of ASM's worship event, with the intent of allowing insight into its worship and music practice. What follows is an application of Grimes's interpretive method for use with rituals, mapping the field of ritual.[47] It supplements the musico-liturgical description through the exegesis of six categories: space, objects, time, sound and language, identity, and action (see Figure 7).

47. Grimes, *Beginnings in Ritual Studies*, 19–32.

Part Two: Turgay Üçal, Agent of Change

Ritual Space
The beautiful nineteenth-century Anglican Church, All Saints Moda (ASM) is located in Moda, on the Asian side of Istanbul. Constructed in 1878, it served a vibrant British community until the mid-1980s, but since 1996, has been used by ASM. Inspiring stain-glass windows in the front, sides and rear of the church provide a visual Bible. The high pointed arches above the chancel are complimented by the decorative hand-carved wooden railing in front of the raised platform, the matching pulpit and pews. The oblong or rectangular building has a single aisle running from the entry through the narthex and nave to the front in a cruciform (Latin Cross) layout. Two benches in the East sector of the cruciform facilitate the male church leadership. A baby grand piano sits directly opposite in the West side of the cruciform. There are eleven rows of pews on either side of the center aisle.
Ritual Objects
Ten objects are associated with the sacrament, including the following: three nickle-plated chalices with three small matching plates and two large plates for two loaves of bread. These elements are used together with a pitcher for the wine and a covered metal container for pre-cut bread into bite-sized pieces. Two Jesus candles sit on either side of the Communion Table. They represent Jesus, the Light of the world. (Turgay uses "Light" as a metaphor with many different interpretations, dependent upon the context).
Ritual Time
The fixed worship event occurs every Sunday morning throughout the liturgical year at 11AM and lasts for approximately one and a half hours. This Western legacy contrasts with the Islamic practice of the combined Friday noon prayers and sermon held at the local mosque.
Ritual Sound and Language
The liturgy includes the language of chant, song, oratory, prayers, and readings. We sing hymns and western choruses, speak ritual responses to Pastor Turgay and/or church leaders, in response to Scripture readings, and throughout the service. Liturgy presupposes literacy in most cases (scripture readings and song lyrics), but some of the liturgy is formulaic and repetitive enough that attendees have it memorized along with the song texts.
Ritual Identity
The roles of pastor, hoca (teacher) and musician are the three most operative roles at ASM. Turgay is all three. His wife, Sibel and pianist Gülmira serve alongside him in leading worship. Assistant pastor, Reşit, and three young man share ministry responsibilities with Turgay. This may include chanting, serving Communion, leading worship and/or preaching.
Ritual Action
Liturgy means "the work of the people." The various kinds of actions performed at ASM as part of the worship event include symbolic actions performed in a fixed place at a fixed recurring interval. It involves actions like recitation, singing, bowing at the waist, gestures, and manipulation of sacred objects with the purpose of expressing a fundamental truth or meaning. It also engages a group of people in unified action to reinforce their common bonds. The quality of action that persists is verticality. Recurrent postures are meant to show honor, glory and worship of our God. We bow and exchange the peace. Standing, sitting and kneeling, each posture has a different meaning. Sitting can be listening, and kneeling, a symbol of humbleness, praise, or adoration. We symbolically receive the Body and Blood of Christ through communion. Following the benediction, we leave in peace to take Christ to the world in our speech and actions.

Figure 7: ASM's Field of Ritual

SUMMARY

In this chapter, I analyzed a Sunday worship event at ASM, revealing the centrality of music to liturgical expression. I also applied Grimes's mapping the field of ritual, a method of interpreting a service. I showed how worship music is an integral part of the interactions that occur during the corporate worship event. Music is also used to represent relationships and to allow the ritual action to take on the character of the whole assembly. Turgay's music making serves to interweave connections among the various parts of the liturgy, including actions and across the verbal character of the entire service. In chapter 6, I present the findings and data analysis that demonstrate the influence of Turgay's songs on the assembly.

6

ASM's Songs in Missional Context

You came to the world to reveal love

and to find me when I was lost.

Come, my Lord, come, my Lord. Come and take my hand.

In your being, I have found my true self.[1]

IN THE PREVIOUS CHAPTER, I provided an analysis of the integral role of music making in the All Saints Moda (ASM) worship event, and I mapped the field of ritual. In this chapter, I focus on the faith community and its songs in the missional context in order to answer the fourth research question: "How do Turgay's songs affectively, cognitively, and behaviorally impact the everyday lives of congregants?"

In chapter 3, I described the methods I used in this experimental research. I now present my research findings, which authenticate a positive correlation between Turgay's songs and strengthened identity and spiritual formation in the lives of ASM assembly members. The first part of my two-tiered research approach involved card sorting: a simple method designed to ascertain the attitude of the assembly members toward Turgay's songs. The follow-up survey, an adaptation of one first used in a similar study,[2] was applied in order to determine the level of influence of Turgay's songs in the assembly member's lives.

---

1. Üçal, Song 73 in this study.
2. King, "Pathways in Christian Music Communication," 353–57.

Appendices J and K, respectively, disclose the card-sorting and survey results. I also gathered data through participant observation. This secondary data source proved useful in confirming the songs' impact on the participants.

The participants stressed again and again that both the pleasing sounds of the music and the meaning of the text were key to determining the appeal of a song. One assembly member affirmed the impact of the sound in the following manner:

> I like the songs, because I really appreciate the music that is in there. There's something about them that carries me away, moves my spirit; that's what I mean—moves my spirit to a different place.[3]

Another assembly member expressed it differently:

> Sometimes I come here without emotions and without feeling connected to the world (actually, separated from the world), and these hymns help me connect. When I hear and sing these hymns, they give me life—just like living water to me, these hymns.[4]

ASM assembly members also emphasized the meaning of the song texts as the main attraction of a song. These songs are significant in confirming members' basic beliefs, strengthening their faith, conveying their spiritual experiences with the Lord, and serving as the stimulus for their joy. The capacity of song to impact congregants in the affective dimension is perceptible among the congregants.

Apparently, there are two sides to a Turgay song that must work within the cognitive dimension. Roberta King writes,

> A song can (1) send a message and also simultaneously (2) express the thoughts or experiences of the participant/singer, allowing them to interact with the message and interpret it in light of their previous or current experiences.[5]

Respondent A. Ö. drew attention to this aspect. She said,

> The hymn "In My Troubles, I Will Call to You" reminds me that there's some sadness all around me—seeds of sadness and grief within my heart. When we sing it, I just feel that my strength is renewed. And it says in the song—without looking back. I'm not

---

3. Respondent 1, interview, December 3, 2014.

4. Respondent 18, interview, November 9, 2014.

5. King, "Pathways in Christian Music Communication," 272.

going to look back at my troubles anymore, because I've given them to God, and I will move forward toward him.[6]

Another participant verified his connection with the song texts:

These songs have deep meanings, and these are the songs I tell myself at home, giving myself the Word of God and reminding myself of the Truth again and again, like a sermon.[7]

Turgay's songs, then, definitely have the potential to speak into the life of an individual, interacting at such an operative level that a sermon is unnecessary, for the proclamation of God's message has already transpired.

King describes the behavioral dimension in communication terminology, stating that it "presupposes the possibility that beliefs and attitudes will be acted upon,"[8] meaning that if a receptor has a positive response to a message that has merged with the person's belief system, "it is most likely that this will be acted upon and a decision made to incorporate the new understandings."[9] These decisions may range from commitment to Christ to participation in church life to application of scripture in their lives.

ASM Christ followers respond positively to the music and are accepting of its message. For the ASM assembly members, much like for the West African Senufo people in King's study, "songs are most effective and significant in effecting change in peoples' lives when they address current, particular problems or dilemmas."[10] Songs are taken seriously as spiritual encounters with God.

Further, nonbelievers also react positively. They are attracted to the musical style and willingly join in either vocally or instrumentally. They sometimes respond emotionally:

I've had friends who came to this church and when singing these hymns, they started weeping. They were moved by the songs and the music.[11]

Participant observation in ASM's worship event confirmed my positive experimental research results. I discovered that assembly members

6. Respondent 6, interview, September 7, 2014.
7. Respondent 16, interview, September 21, 2014.
8. King, "Pathways," 273.
9. King, "Pathways," 273.
10. King, "Pathways," 283.
11. Respondent 14, interview, April 27, 2014.

wholeheartedly participated and appeared to thrive in their Christian and social identities[12] as they worshiped and experienced greater understanding and meaning through musico-liturgical inculturation. Turgay's songs reveal a broad spectrum of concepts and experiences of God expressed in a common theological mode.

In the words of Peter Craigie: "It is a theology or knowledge of God which emerges out of a life lived in relationship with God."[13] In his book *Constructing Local Theologies*, Robert Schreiter explains,

> One cannot speak of a community developing a local theology without its being filled with the Spirit and working under the power of the gospel . . . Another way of speaking about this context created by the movement of the Spirit and by the power of the gospel in a community is that it creates a certain spirituality among the believers.[14]

That spirituality in the ASM community provided the necessary framework to develop culturally related theology. Turgay did it intuitively for himself as well as the ASM believers. It has not always been so.

While committed to church ministry at the age of twenty-four (1986), Turgay did not grasp Christianity as his own until 2008, when his friendship with a Jewish rabbi encouraged him to reflect deeply on Jesus's lifestyle of simplicity and compassion. Turgay writes,

> God gave me fresh understanding of the Gospels and I felt I was really engaging with the Living Christ. It was a transforming experience to hear Jesus's voice more directly and not only as he has been interpreted and handed down through the ages through various ethnic traditions, cultural interpretations, and theological systems. Suddenly, this changed the picture and brought me joy. The Bible became my own and wasn't just words on a page or concepts to be taught and grasped. My spirituality was enriched and my perspective improved, as I began to sit at the feet of Jesus.[15]

After much study, prayer, and reflection on Jesus, Turgay envisioned a new way of relating to his context and his church. His people began to

---

12. Brown, *Social Identity Theory*, 745–78.

13. Craigie, *Psalms 1–50*, 40.

14. Schreiter, *Constructing Local Theologies*, 24.

15. Üçal, "From Church Planting to Human Planting," 2.

put hospitality front and center, welcoming their neighbors into their Messianic Center[16] and worship services. Turgay notes,

> Our worship style, outreach, and discipleship began to mesh with our goals of engaging and connecting more deeply with our surrounding community and culture in Istanbul.[17]

The worship style reflects their Middle Eastern culture, and it embodies Turgay's local theology.

WORSHIP

Elaborating on Jesus's promise to prepare many rooms, Turgay stated, "Our Father has many rooms, and All Saints Moda is one of them."[18] Be that as it may, Turgay understands that not everyone will comprehend or appreciate the ASM worship practice. For one thing, he prohibits the use of electronic musical instruments in worship. This is consistent with other faiths in Turkey: Judaism, Orthodoxy, and Islam. However, the liturgy comprises more than music.

Songs, rituals, symbols, and creeds help believers establish their identities and where they belong, plus these orientate believers in relation to one another. For example, one female respondent confirmed this through the following statement:

> I have an Alevi background, so I have similar instruments to what is used in this music and this style of singing. Because of that, I have familiarity with these hymns already, and I feel very close to them.[19]

Another respondent attests to this:

> These songs help explain what I believe about God as my Father, God as our Lord, God as part of us, and God over all of his creation, including everyone else who exists in this world.[20]

---

16. The church office functions as the church ministry center.
17. Üçal, "From Church Planting to Human Planting," 3.
18. Üçal, interview, July 15, 2013.
19. Respondent 10, interview, January 11, 2015.
20. Respondent 2, interview, October 13, 2013.

Turgay concluded, "I look at our culture and say this is the way forward.[21] All Saints Moda fits Allen Tippett's depiction of an indigenous church:

> When the indigenous people of a community think of the Lord as their own, not a foreign Christ; when they do things as unto the Lord meeting the cultural needs around them, worshiping in patterns they understand; when their congregation functions in participation in a body which is structurally indigenous, then you have an *indigenous* church.[22]

The gospel-centered, mission-shaped church community called All Saints Moda is appropriate to its immediate surroundings because of its musico-liturgical inculturation. Drawing from his spiritual journey, Turgay stated,

> Changing religions for a Muslim creates turmoil in the spirit, because it is not just a personal thing; you are turning your back on your family. And if you are a national, it feels like you are turning your back on your nation, because Turks connect religion to nationality, per the slogan "To be a Turk is to be a Muslim." If you are turning your back on your faith, you are turning your back on your nation, on being a Turk or Kurd or Alevi, and you are turning your back on your family.[23]

In contrast, at All Saints Moda, believers with Muslim backgrounds (MBBs) have a sense of belonging. They feel at home. Perhaps it would be helpful to compare a few Sufi worship practices with ASM's liturgy to understand how converts from Islam/Sufism to Christianity connect with the worship service and think of the church as a Messianic *dergah*.[24]

Within Islam, the 700-year-old Mevlevi branch that originated in Konya, Turkey, is undoubtedly the most well-known one as a result of its practice of whirling (the *sema*). The *Sema* is the main worship practice in the whirling dervish ceremony. It is also a time for the *semazens* to nourish the soul through devotional hearing of the subtle sounds of the cosmos as they whirl in a circle. This corresponds to ASM's first liturgical

---

21. Üçal, interview, July 15, 2013.

22. Tippett, *Solomon Islands Christianity*, 381.

23. Üçal, interview, July 15, 2013.

24. A *dergah* is a Sufi lodge, a gathering place where dervishes (members of a Sufi religious order) seek knowledge through dialogue with a *sheikh* (Sufi spiritual leader).

section that focuses on hearing God's Word: songs, Scripture readings, and the sermon. See Table 6.

Table 6: Comparison of Sufi Worship Practices to ASM Liturgy[25]

Sufi		Christian		
Sema	"Hearing" Listening to the sounds of the cosmos	21st c	Worship songs Scripture Sermon	"Hearing" from God in word and song
Secde	"Prostrating" A posture of praying with face to the floor	1st c	Prayers after the Sermon	"Bow Downs" Preparation of the heart
Zikr	"Remembrance" Repetition of God's names is considered one of the best ways to gain spiritual enlightenment, a feeling of peace, and to strengthen faith.	1st c	The Lord's Table	"Remembrance" Partaking of communion elements is a reminder of Christ's great sacrifice on the cross, but it also is a reminder that he is coming again.

The *Secde*, a second core Sufi worship practice, involves prostration before God, similar to ASM's "bow downs" section after the sermon. This twenty-first century practice includes three prayers and a statement of faith, in preparation for the Lord's Table: (1) a prayer of glorification (2) The Lord's Prayer (3) the *Amidah* prayer, and (4) chanting of 1 Tim 3:16.

In the *Zikr*, dervishes recite the names of God in continual repetition. This literally means remembrance and recollection of Him. With this spiritual exercise, they seek to become closer to God. Their worship practice has characteristics in common with the third and last section of ASM's liturgy: The Lord's Table. It is a reminder of what Christ did for us on the cross. It is also a confession of faith. Those who participate silently confess before the congregation, "I believe in Jesus Christ as Savior and Redeemer, and I believe he is coming again."

As demonstrated earlier, Pastor Turgay carefully evaluates the religious practices/forms he integrates into the All Saints Moda worship practice. In addition to those he retains with little adjustment, there also are practices that Turgay strives to recast. In each case, these adopted practices and forms are selected because of their application to molding the Christian identity of the ASM assembly. Sharing some excellent insight, Charles Kraft writes,

25. Üçal, interview, May 15, 2015.

> In this way, Christians, working in terms of already existing cultural patterns and processes but with God's will as their reference point and his Spirit to empower them, may have an important influence on the direction in which the culture is changed. And one important result of such directed change will be the transformation of certain of the cultural patterns and processes to serve Christian ends more adequately.[26]

On the other hand, as Donald McGavran notes, "It is seldom recognized that transformation has never historically attained total conversion to true Christianity and probably never will."[27] There are limits to cultural changes.

Even though ASM shares many practices/forms with other Christian churches, others are deliberately not used. These are the practices that, in Turgay's opinion, attach an undesirable and foreign identity to the church. He is not convinced that such practices are scriptural, as they increase the church's "otherness" and create barriers between the church assembly and the local community. His goal is to inspire a seeker's nascent faith and help shape the faith of people impacted by the gospel message.

The inculturation of ASM's worship rites came about as a result of a "supracultural reference point" (God) for cultural change,[28] thus creating something new—an innovative liturgy and an indigenous hymnody (see Figure 8). At the forefront of Turgay's mind is how national Christians in Turkey can express their faith in ways that bring the reality of Christ's incarnation into the heart of Anatolian culture. He wants them to feel fully themselves.[29]

---

26. Kraft, *Christianity in Culture*, 64.

27. Kraft, *Christianity in Culture*, 64.

28. Kraft, *Christianity in Culture*, 63. "When people shift (convert) from a cultural to a supracultural reference point, the assumption that this is the best thing to do becomes a part of their worldview. It then partially or fully replaces the previous reference point in terms of which such decision was made."

29. The identity of various ethnic groups within Turkey (remnant of the Ottoman Empire) is linked tightly to their lineage, be it Kurdish, Armenian, Laz, Turkish, Jewish, Greek, and so on.

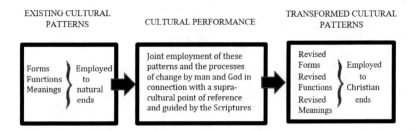

Figure 8: Christian Transformational Change[30]

Toward that end, Turgay has been and continues to be prayerful in his discernment of how musico-liturgical elements are incorporated. Indirectly affirming this approach, Brian Schrag states, "We have seen that the more a community appropriately values its own culture, the more the kingdom of God is likely to thrive."[31] Turgay's vision has proven to be fruitful, bringing about maturity and growth of his assembly in its local setting.

SPIRITUAL FORMATION

The expression of worship at All Saints Moda is a contextualized liturgy. It reflects the essential "pluriformity of Christian liturgy,"[32] embodying Turgay's local theology. As Mary McGann describes in her study,[33] when a congregation actively participates in a public celebration of liturgy, they engage in a deeply relational experience, identifying who they are spiritually as a church in relation to each other, the rest of the human family, and to God. He is the heart of all theological happenings.

Believers at ASM feel fully Christian and fully *Istanbuli* when they sing Turgay's hymns. His works are effectively aiding in the development of the next generation of ministry leaders at ASM, including the three young men currently studying with him.[34]

---

30. Kraft, *Christianity in Culture*, 63.

31. Schrag and Krabill, *Creating Local Arts Together*, 25.

32. McGann, *Exploring Music as Worship and Theology*, 14.

33. McGann, *Exploring Music as Worship and Theology*, 16–17.

34. Üçal, *Şabat Ayini İlahileri* (Sabbath Ritual hymns), first hymnbook.

LEADERSHIP DEVELOPMENT

Key issues in leadership development center on character (being). Character reflects the heart of a leader, while soul work develops the leader's Christlikeness. This issue is reflected in Turgay's songs. For example, one male respondent confirmed,

> These songs are about life on earth, about day-to-day struggles, about living in this world, about struggles that we face, struggling with them and overcoming them. So, they are about how to live life, and the reality of life.[35]

The glory of hymnody, according to Erik Routley, "is in its power for converting unbelief, strengthening faith, and binding together the Christian community in the disciplined charity of which singing together is a symbol."[36] Leaders-in-waiting at ASM must be familiar with and able to lead Turgay's indigenous worship songs and others similar in character.

After people are discipled and are ready to teach, Turgay encourages them to go into their community and "imitate what we're doing here."[37] He instructs them to use the Scriptures and ASM's common prayer booklet and just spend time with people. He knows that is how God draws people to bow down and glorify him—people from Orthodox, Muslim, and secular backgrounds.[38] New leaders at ASM are prepared to serve in their own cultural settings.

The All Saints Moda assembly has found that the authentic, honest approach works well in their community and context. "While many Westerners prefer to impart knowledge intellectually rather than in the context of relationship, most of the world has a strong cultural emphasis on relationships."[39]

WITNESS

"We have many stories of lives changed through the gospel, and relationship continues to be the primary way we reach non-believers in Istanbul,"[40]

---

35. Respondent 8, interview, January 11, 2015.

36. Routley, *Hymns and Human Life*, 307.

37. Üçal, "From Church Planting to Human Planting," 5.

38. Üçal, "From Church Planting to Human Planting," 5.

39. Üçal, "From Church Planting to Human Planting," 3.

40. Üçal, "From Church Planting to Human Planting," 5.

Part Two: Turgay Üçal, Agent of Change

Turgay says. Through samples from my research data (Appendix K), let us listen in on the impact of his songs:

> When I first came here [ASM], I heard the hymns, and I would weep almost every time, and that's when I made a decision that I have to come here. I need to come here. This is where I accepted Christ into my heart. The music is very important, because as Turks we don't have anything in our own language where we can talk to the Father Creator, and we don't know how to call out to him, because everything is done in Arabic. Because this is in Turkish, it automatically has a connection within our hearts, that hole we could not fill with Arabic. Now we are able to do it in Turkish, with our own language and music, and are able to refer to God as Father, our Creator, in this way.[41]

A similar experience was shared by another congregant:

> I really like "Listen Closely, O My Heart," because that was the first hymn that I heard before I became a believer. I came here and I heard about God's sweet voice, you know, that small voice that the Bible talks about. And when I heard that hymn was written here, that especially touched me more, knowing that it was local.[42]

Emotionally, cognitively, and behaviorally, people are moved by Turgay's songs. Reviewing the church's growth, Turgay explains that in Istanbul, many people learn about this assembly without any contact with a mission or missionary. Several people who are now mature Christ followers came to faith in a variety of astonishing ways. Some were visitors to the museum across the street from ASM who also wanted to see the inside of the historic Anglican building completed in 1878. Others were attendees of recitals and concerts held in the facility by various school and professional musical groups. Architecture students from a nearby university came to observe the various ways a church can be expressed. In some cases, it has been simple curiosity about the Protestant worship experience.

Personal Evangelism

In personal evangelism, Turgay leans toward a gradual process; without pushing and prodding, he gently encourages individuals to enter the kingdom. People in his sphere of ministry generally come to Christ "in a

41. Respondent 3, interview, November 9, 2014.
42. Respondent 12, interview, November 1, 2014.

118

natural way," through shared life experiences in community or as a result of face-to-face dialogue in the church office or in an informal setting. Altar calls following a sermon—an evangelical phenomenon beginning in the late 1800s—is not a part of ASM's worship events. Let us listen to K.E.'s testimony:

> I've been attending ASM for the last ten months and made a decision to follow Jesus in the past four months. I was thinking that religion is not Islam or Christianity, but Judaism. But I've come to believe more in Jesus. I'm going to get baptized before Christmas. There's no pressure. For ten months I've been reading, looking, and investigating, and this is my decision. But I'm going to be baptized because Jesus was baptized. What I know is that I trust in Jesus, and that's how I want to live my life from now on.[43]

Turgay is currently teaching two separate groups of his wife's unsaved friends, an eight-member group from Sibel's alma mater that comes to the church office on a weekly basis for two-hour discussions on the Christian faith, and a group of Sibel's artist colleagues with whom she shares a cooperative art studio. Turgay has just begun commuting to their co-op by car to share the good news. The alma mater friends have been attending Turgay's classes for the past three years, and two have become believers.[44]

Community Ministry

It is an understatement to say that sharing the gospel message inside the Islamic world is a challenging task. In Phil Parshall's book *The Last Great Frontier: Essays on Muslim Evangelism,* Bill and Jane, unidentified missionaries, state, "If the status quo is to change, a new way must be found whereby Muslims can come to Christ in the context of their own culture and community."[45]

Acutely aware that God had strategically placed them in their location to make a difference, Turgay and other members of the ASM assembly began prayerfully assessing how the church could effectively reach out to the surrounding community. Eventually, two creative options best suited

---

43. Respondent 8, interview, October 22, 2013. This respondent accepted Christ as Savior, was baptized as intended, and today faithfully attends ASM as of October 15, 2018.

44. Üçal, interview, September 11, 2018. This group continues to meet each week, Turgay tells me that a third member of the class has come to faith.

45. Parshall, *Last Great Frontier,* 178.

for the local setting became impressed upon their minds: hospitality and community outreach events. It has been said that "hospitality is one of the cornerstones of the Turkish way of life."[46]

Hospitality

Hospitality, in general, can change people. It tends to soften hearts and focus people on the right things, particularly Spirit-infused hospitality. Thus, ASM is modeling Christian love and acceptance to the larger community by opening its doors Monday through Thursday between 10:00 a.m. and 4:00 p.m. so people have an opportunity to experience God in a safe environment.

The Barış Manço mansion, a famous pop artist museum, sits across the street from ASM. Of the thirty-six thousand visitors annually received by the museum from all over the country, one-third (twelve thousand) walk across the street to visit ASM, also considered a museum. Some people enter out of curiosity, having never been inside a church, while others (Orthodox Christians and folk Islamic practitioners) come to light a candle in the sand-filled candleholder just inside the entrance.[47] Typically they will sit for a moment of silent prayer and meditation before leaving.

As much as possible, Turgay and his office assistants make themselves available for questions or discussion throughout their four-day office week.[48] New Testaments and prayer books are free for the taking from the racks on the back of the pews; ASM gives away approximately two thousand prayer books and one thousand New Testaments (İncils) each year. True hospitality is a spiritual ministry about welcoming all in the name of Christ.

The church also makes the room available for art shows by various community art organizations, university music concerts, and private music teacher recitals. In addition, the church hosts weddings and receptions throughout the year. The receptions are held in the back garden of ASM's church office conveniently located next door to the historic building.

46. Muyan Suites, Muyan website, line 9.

47. The All Saints Moda assembly is responsible for maintaining the traditional features of the church throughout the church year. This includes a fresh supply of candles for visitors near the large sand-filled candle holder.

48. A security TV screen in the church office alerts ASM's church staff when visitors enter the sanctuary next door.

Musical Outreach Events

Part of ASM's outreach is its own mixture of choral and instrumental concerts that provide free or low-cost cultural events to the greater community through a "soft-evangelism"[49] approach. God speaks to human hearts through beauty, and the arts are a means of revelation in the world.

In 2016, Turgay created a new opportunity for choral-loving[50] local music makers to gather every Sunday afternoon and sing favorite traditional Turkish art songs (*şarklar*). This came with the promise of a concert performance following two months of rehearsal. After fixing a placard to ASM's front metal fence announcing the commencement of weekly rehearsals at the church (open to all who love to sing), the ticketed[51] event did not disappoint. It drew a full house of young and old, mostly local people who had never before been inside a church sanctuary. Smiling faces were everywhere.[52]

Unlike any other choral concert I have experienced, every choir member had a solo, and the audience sang along with the choir, even the instrumentalists and choir director! This was amazing. With a seven-piece ensemble of combined traditional and Western instruments accompanying the twenty-two-voice chorale, it truly was an impactful evening.[53] The positive response was such that the rehearsals continued and an even more successful concert (larger performance group, more instrumentalists, and a

49. Turgay says of human planting, "It's less about religion and more about touching people on a human level, giving them a desire to know more about Christ Jesus" (Üçal, "From Church Planting to Human Planting," 3).

50. Choral music in Turkey is never sung in parts but is instead characterized by the simultaneous variation on a single melodic line: a style called *heterophony*. All voices and instruments perform the melody.

51. The price of a ticket was equivalent of five dollars (US) to cover the costs of the professional choral conductor and instrumentalists: kanun, ney, two ouds, clarinet, violin, and Turkish hand drum.

52. This account was written shortly after ASM's first concert. Turgay has since created an ongoing choral concert series, drawing participants and a full house to performances from the surrounding neighborhood for the past three years. I attended three of them while living in Istanbul. The series was still ongoing two years later.

53 ASM is a lovely performance venue for medium-sized audiences, and Turgay has made it available to the public for those purposes, including the Istanbul evangelical youth group's monthly gatherings, Western classical instrument and vocal concerts, choral groups, string ensembles, and area-wide art shows. Turgay's expectation is that God's chosen ones will return on a Sunday morning in response to the prompting of the Holy Spirit.

larger audience) was performed three months later. These concerts are now listed in the church calendar as three-times-a-year events.

ASM's outreach of love toward its local community may be the most impactful thing the assembly can do initially. They do good to their neighbors in practical ways that meet felt needs.

Turgay has a biblical worldview, believing his primary reason for existence is to love and serve God. Boldly sharing who he is as a follower of Christ, he is challenging in witness, whether in word or song, both publicly and privately. He witnesses to God's love and grace. In Song 46, he proclaims the following:

> O heavens, O earth
>
> Our God is everything to us
>
> We were all sinful at heart
>
> We were mired deep in sin
>
> Through this pardon that came from heaven above
>
> Grace cleansed us.[54]

Turgay's writings are penned from the perspective of more than thirty years of pastoral ministry, and are filled with fully formed opinions about how to share Christ authentically in a Muslim context. They represent the heart of his ministry, which he describes as "human planting."

Human Planting

What does human planting mean? Spiritually and figuratively, Turgay claims that this concept "is a reaction against the kind of church planting that relies heavily on programs, western methods, formulas, buildings, and money as a way of pushing ministry forward."[55] He is convinced that 'that' kind of church planting sees the big picture rather than the person, numbers over relationships, and opportunity over engagement.

Human planting focuses on reaching out to spiritually needy people, leading them from a basic animal level of *egoism* (an attitude of "it's all about me") to Christ and transformation into the image of God. This transformation is for the good of the seeker and is from friend to friend, not to fulfill quotas or to reach a program goal. Turgay has faith that this

---

54. Üçal, Song 46 in this study.

55. Üçal, "From Church Planting to Human Planting," 2.

approach will yield great Kingdom rewards. He knows that if a person changes, nations change.[56] What additional evidence does one require to fully embrace inculturation?

Turgay's work reveals him as an agent of change. As God's representative in ministry and mission, he is fulfilling God's purposes through musico-liturgical inculturation, and ultimately, facilitating transformational change into Christlikeness.

SUMMARY AND CONCLUSION

In this chapter, I examined why and how these song texts move the people who sing them. Briefly, my conclusions are the following: (1) Turgay's indigenous songs are a primary vehicle of the local culture—its heritage of language and melody. God repeatedly reveals himself in its expressive manner of enactment and its social and faith-related memory. (2) The congregation's theology is embedded in a unique musico-liturgical worship practice. It is spoken, chanted, enacted, and sung. (3) Turgay aggressively pursues the biblical mandate to make disciples. Through inculturation of disciple-making, Spirit-filled worship at ASM, he is a strategic part of the greater story of what God is doing in Turkey and throughout the world.

---

56. Üçal, "From Church Planting to Human Planting," 2.

Praying Twice: Modes and Means

7

Culturally Tuned Music

> For Turks who believe in Jesus, that Sufi music is just really important. It encapsulates everything together. I'm a believer, but I'm also a Turk, and I don't want to leave an empty space. I want my beliefs to interface with my culture. I see that Turgay is creating a new thing—a believing Turkish model.[1]

AFTER FOCUSING ON TURGAY'S personal pilgrimage as well as his music within the setting of a church community in a missional context, I now analyze the *repertoires* and *aesthetics* of Turgay's worship songs, two components of music-culture.[2] They encompass style, genres, texts, composition, transmission, movement, and material culture. Gaetano Lotrecchiano states, "Each cultural musical system must be understood on its own terms, with its unique aesthetic preferences and its own internal referents of meaning."[3] Extending his line of thinking, Vida Chenoweth reasons that "unless we believe that individual cultures have a unique and valid contribution to make to Christian worship, the significance of ethnic music—along with all other means of expression—will escape us entirely."[4] Attention to each musical dimension is vital for an adequate understanding of how the worship songs at All Saints Moda (ASM) and its surrounding music-culture interacts.

1. Respondent 18, interview, June 27, 2013.
2. Titon, *Worlds of Music*, 20.
3. Lotrecchiano, "Ethnomusicology and the Study of Musical Change," 119.
4. Chenoweth, "Spare Them Western Music," lines 20–23.

Part Three: Praying Twice: Modes and Means

STYLE

The style of Turgay's worship songs may be described as *monophonic*. Regardless of the number of singers or accompanying instruments, the songs feature a single melody line. Instead, instrumentalists or vocalists that perform together freely improvise and embellish the melody appropriate for his or her specific instrument, creating an intricate and resonant soundscape called heterophony ("different voices").

The aesthetic of the music comes from the combination of timbres and unique ornamentation. Additionally, the vocal aesthetic includes elements of vibrato, in which the pitch is slowly shaken.[5] As per Titon, "Together, style and aesthetics create a recognizable sound that a group understands as its own."[6] How is style different from genre?

GENRE

The term *genre* designates a category of repertoire, a shared set of musical norms. In the case of Turkish makam music (TMM), it refers to the subcategories of (1) classical Turkish music (TCM) in the Ottoman period, from 1299 to 1923, and (2) Turkish *sanat* music (TSM), an art song form that came into vogue starting in 1923 after the secular Turkish Republic was established. TCM has become the music of choice for a growing number of Turkish citizens today, according to Eliot Bates, author of the book *Music in Turkey*. He writes the following:

> Since the early 2000s, *Klasik Türk Müziği* has seen perhaps its greatest resurgence ever, as it has become popular with urban Muslim youth movements as a morally acceptable alternative to the risqué lyrics and alcohol-serving performane contexts of pop music . . . Early recordings of *Klasik Türk Müziği* have survived. These recordings have recently come to have an unprecedented significance as the sole exemplars of proper performance on several instruments, and they continue to be scrutinized, analyzed, and mimicked today by younger generations of musicians. In Istanbul today, Turkish-language TSM has supplanted most other art music genres.[7]

5. Several ornamental notes sung to one syllable of text, like in plainsong or blues singing.

6. Titon, *Worlds of Music*, 27.

7. Bates, *Music in Turkey*, 49–50.

What are the implications of this recent phenomenon for the Protestant church in Turkey? As for ASM, how do they relate to Turgay's partiality for worship songs in traditional Turkish genres? He has created eighty worship songs in three different music genres (see Figure 9). Of that total number, sixty-eight are TSM; nonetheless, Turgay describes fifty-two of those as 'Sufi songs' or hymns (*ilahiler*)[8] because the texts are prayers. Eleven are CTM and one falls into the folk music category (TFM). Turkish folk music is modal, but not considered TMM.[9]

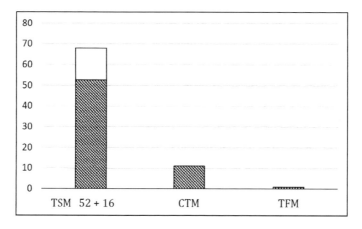

Figure 9: The Three Genres of Turgay's Hymns

Turgay's contribution to ASM's repertoire is a significant part of the assembly's total number of worship songs. In the church's music there are three self-determined genres of music: (1) translated Western songs (TW) (2) Turkish makam music (TMM) and (3) Turkish folk music (TFM). This mixture reflects Istanbul's East-West context—social, historical, cultural, political, religious, and familial.

The music rotates on a ten-week cycle calendar (Appendix G), incorporating material of each genre. I interject here that the calendar is a fluid guide

8. Sufi music is the worship music of mystic brotherhoods or *tarikats* (Islamic fraternity and religious orders) like the famous Mevlevi Sufi order founded by the followers of Rumi, a thirteenth-century poet and Islamic theologian. Whirling (or Sufi turning) is still practiced today by the dervishes of the Mevlevi order.

9. Turkish folk music has its own style, forms and instruments. For example, folksong melodies are called *ayak* (foot) and have patterns with no rules of progression. Many have only part of a melodic pattern. They have similarities closer to medieval church modes than do makam-s.

on any given Sunday. Turgay is led by the Spirit, meaning he will change the direction of the service when so moved, sometimes inserting a spontaneous song, sometimes leading the congregation in public prayers (Turgay refers to this as "Korean style"),[10] or sometimes asking worshipers to meditate for a few moments. The calendar yields to the Holy Spirit.

The translated worship songs typically are familiar ones that visiting Western believers will recognize. A soft ballad song form in 4/4 time is customary. The translations, however, normally do not fit well with the melody. Alterations to the melody and the rhythm made to accommodate the differences in the number of syllables and the textual emphasis give the music an unnatural feel. It sounds different, too, because the assembly "Turkifies" the melody. If not a trained musician, a local tends to sing with a nasal tone and to adlib passing tones between pitches.

Worship songs in the traditional folksong format are created by a few national composers. Short and modal, the texts fit nicely with the music.

Turkish instruments such as the oud (lute), *kanun* (zither), and *ney* (flute) are more appropriate for accompanying Turgay's songs; but since no one at the church plays a Turkish instrument (other than him), the piano provides the accompaniment. Gülmira, the Russian pianist, beautifully harmonizes each of the genres with simple chords. Congregants, however, do not break into part singing during musical worship, because harmony is not part of the normative music-making experience in the culture.

The vocal music style (including chanting, also known as *cantillation* or *intoned speech*) is unlike that of any other Protestant church in Turkey. Added to Turgay's solo chanting of Scripture at the beginning of the worship event is the congregation supplemental chanting of prayers (responsive, and in unison) during the liturgy. Westerners pick up on these unique practices and comment on them. Chanting is a key mode of Middle Eastern ritual expressiveness. In addition to shaping the liturgy, these vocal forms powerfully affect how all other elements of the liturgical action are experienced, and they assist in the meaning-making that takes place in ASM's worship. What about the differences between Eastern and Western musics? Why do Turkish melodies sound peculiar to the Western ear?

10. Many Korean workers in Turkey are charismatic in their worship style, including the practice of everyone praying aloud at once.

Pitch—Makam

Unlike the Western tonal system founded on the tempered system that includes twelve equal semitones in a scale, the Turkish melodic tradition involves twenty-four tones in the octave set in microtonal spaces and identified as the "twenty-four-note system."[11] Additionally, the pitches are transposed a perfect fourth above Western notation. This latter phenomenon can present both aural and visual challenges to Western musicians at first. For example, the 440 Hz frequency of A1 on the piano is the same as D2 in Turkish music. Musicians of Turkey have been using this transposed notation since the 1930s.

Moreover, microtonal tones sound strange to Western ears, as those microtonal pitches are not in their musical vocabulary. In Ottoman-Turkish music theory, it is possible to divide a whole step into nine equal commas and a half step into four equal commas. Thus, a tone has four possibilities of comma formations: four, five, eight, and nine. The closest comparison to a half-step interval (4.5) in the Western scale is the Turkish semitone, which has an unequal distance of four commas. As a result of these different mathematical representations, the Western octave contains fifty-four commas, whereas the Eastern music contain fifty-three. Described in a different way, the Western semitone equals 100 cents and the tone equals 200 cents, whereas the Eastern semitone equals 90 cents and the tone equals 204 cents.

To indicate European notation for these new intervals, ranging from one to twelve-thirteen commas, it was necessary to create additional names and symbols.[12] See Table 7. The Turkish interval symbols are represented by capitalized letters, and their koma values are identified as follows: F (one koma), B (four komas), S (five komas), K (eight komas), and T (a whole step). When two notes create an interval larger than a whole step, the letter "A" is used to indicate this augmented second interval (A12 or A13 komas), depending upon the makam.[13]

---

11. Aydemir, *Turkish Music Makam Guide*, 17.

12. Signell, *Makam: Modal Practice in Art Music*, 3.

13. Chanting and a cappella singing during the ASM worship service negates the need for synthesis of Ottoman-Turkish melodies and Western harmony.

Table 7: Turkish Interval Names, Komas, and Symbols

Interval Names	Komas	Symbols
koma or fazia	1	F
bakiye	4	B
kücük mücenneb	5	S
büyük mücenneb	8	K
tanini	9	T
artik ikili	12 - 13	A12 - A13

Along with these additional intervals are corresponding accidental symbols. In contrast to the European system, Turkish classical music contains six additional accidentals: three sharps and three flats.[14] However, added pitches go hand-in-hand with issues of intonation. "These details of intonation are frequent issues of discussion among musicians," according to ethnomusicologist, Martin Greve,[15] as intonation is often a personal matter of opinion.

Another basic difference between the two music systems are the general rules regarding major and minor patterns that apply to all scales in Western-based music, which is not the case in Turkish makam music. There are no general principles that apply to all makamlar (plural), so Turkish musicians study each makam separately. The preferred method to learn Turkish makam music is *meşk*—the one-on-one traditional education for combining study of "theory, practice, repertoire and performance techniques taught in a holistic approach."[16]

A simple version of Reinhard and Stokes' explanation of Turkish art music is as follows.[17] The sequence of tones in a makam (scale-like pattern) comprises one *pentachord* (a series of five tones) and a *tetrachord* (a series of four tones) or vice versa in various combinations that allow for many possibilities of melodic patterns. We can categorize makam-s as composition rules in three groups: basic makam-s (thirteen makam-s are normally used today), transposed makam-s (created by transposing the basic makam-s to other tones), and compound makam-s (combinations of two or more

14. Savas, "Accidentals of Turkish Classical Music," example 1.
15. Greve, *Makamsız: Individualization of Traditional Music*, 261.
16. Greve, *Makamsız: Individualization of Traditional Music*, 16.
17. Reinhard and Stokes, "Turkey IV: Art Music," 9–19.

makam-s). Composition rules further include guidelines for the up and down movements of the melody, the first and last notes of the piece, and the range and order of notes.

The twelve makamlar in this study of Turgay's hymns encompass the following: Rast, Hicaz, Nihavend, Hicazkâr, Segâh, Uşşak, Mahur, Kürdî, Hüseyni, Bûselik, Nikriz, Saba, and Tahir. See his makam frequency of use in Figure 10.

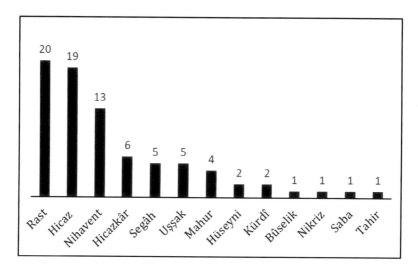

Figure 10: Makam Frequency of Use

Turgay prefers to use the following three makamlar in his compositions: Rast (twenty songs), Hicaz (nineteen songs), and Nihavent (thirteen songs). The Rast is one of the oldest in existence. It is especially familiar to Turgay and the other residents of Turkey, because the Muslim call to prayer (or *ezan*), which normally takes place in the early afternoon *(ikindi)*, in addition to the day's final call to prayer in the evening *(vatsi)* are recited using the Rast makam. Additionally, it is associated with Turkish classical music and urban popular music on radio, TV, and nightlife entertainment. Thus, the Rast makam resonates with Muslim culture in both rural and urban contexts. Its scale pattern consists of the following sequence: T (one whole step), K (eight komas), S (five komas), T (one whole step), T (one whole step), K (eight komas), and S (five komas). See Figure 11.

Figure 11: Rast Makam[18]

Turgay's second most frequently used makam, the Hicaz, resonates with the culture because Turkish mothers/nannies traditionally sing lullabies in this tonality to infants and young children.[19] Its scale pattern consists of the following sequence: S (five komas), A (augmented 2nd), S (five komas), T (one whole step), S (five komas), A (augmented 2nd), and S (five komas). See Figure 12.

Figure 12: Hicaz Makam

Located in third place in terms of Turgay's makam frequency of use in his works is the Nihavent scale pattern. It is similar to the Western key of g minor. See Figure 13. for the precise sequence of letter symbols and intervals linked to the Nihavent makam: T (one whole step), B (four komas), T (one whole step), T (one whole step), B (four komas), T (one whole step), and T (one whole step).

Figure 13: Nihavent Makam

18. See Appendix E for Turgay's hymn, *Kurtuluş Pınarlarına*, originally composed in the Rast makam and transposed into the Western key of E.

19. Üçal, interview, July 15, 2013.

The brevity of these compositions is such that there is no need for modulation to other makamlar such as those that occur in longer works. Turgay's melodic style includes both syllabic and melismatic settings of texts, which contain melodic ornamentation and *glissandos* (slides) between intervals of a skip both ascending and descending. A *skip* is any interval between a third and larger. The rhythmic complement to melodic rhythm in classical music is *usul*, a fundamental rhythmic sequence that supplements the melodic rhythm and may help shape the entire structure of a work.

Time—Usul[20]

In defining the usul, Karl Signell writes, "A usul is a repeated rhythmic cycle, roughly equivalent to the Western 'measure,' but closer in concept to the *tala* of India."[21] Usul-s are known by their names rather than by their meters and are divided into two categories: major and minor usul-s. The minor usul-s (*küçük*) are those that range from two to fifteen beats, while the majors (*büyük*) include sixteen to 128 beats. The majority of Turkish usul-s have rhythmic patterns that move across the bar. Even so, Turgay prefers the minor usul-s.

Traditional vocables are linked with various combinations of these rhythmic patterns (for example, Dum, Du-um, Tek, Tek-ya, Teke, Te-ek) that represent different combinations of stronger and weaker intensities and durations. On the occasions when Turkish musicians or percussion instruments such as the *bendir* (hand drum) are unavailable, the pulsations are defined by striking the knees with the hands, the right hand on the right knee (Dum) and the left hand on the left (Tek).

What follows is a brief description of Turgay's three most frequently used usul patterns, the *Sofyan*, *Semâî*, and *Düyek*. They account for almost 85 percent of the eighty works in this study.

Fifty-two worship songs are written with the Sofyan rhythmic pattern (see Figure 14). One of the shorter usul-s and similar to the Western 4/4 time, it features a four-beat rhythm with three strokes. The count begins with two pulses with the right hand: long (Du-um) and one pulse on beat three (Te), followed by another pulse with the left hand on beat four (Ke). Note stems up are cues for the right hand. Stems down are cues for the left.

---

20. *Usul* is singular and *usul-s*, plural.

21. Signell, *Makam: Modal Practice in Turkish Art Music*, 16.

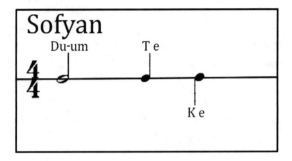

Figure 14: Sofyan Usul

Turgay's second most frequently occurring usul is the Semâî, a popular pattern in Turkish classical music that is found in both slow and lively tempos. Used less frequently in Turgay's hymnody, ten of the eighty-song collection share this rhythmic pattern (see Figure 15). It begins with a right-handed pulse on the first beat, followed by two left-handed pulses on beats two and three.

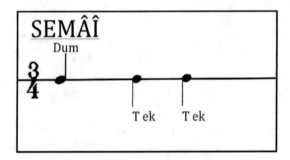

Figure 15: Semâî Usul

The Düyek usul is the third most frequently occurring rhythmic pattern in Turgay's hymnody. It is used only seven times (see Figure 16). This usul, comprised of eight pulses in each measure, starts off with a short downbeat with the right hand, followed by a long and short pulse with the left on beats two and four. The right hand then completes the rhythmic pattern, with two long pulses on beats five and seven.

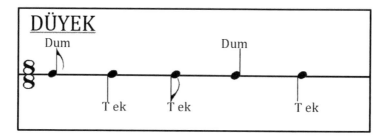

Figure 16: Düyek Usul

In addition to the top three selections, Turgay also draws on seven other rhythmic patterns to a lesser degree, all of which are categorized within the minor group of usul-s: *Aksak* (three); *Sofyan-Düyek* (two); *Serbest*, which means "freely," (two); *Müsemmem* (one); *Oynak* (one); *Sengin Semâî* (one); and *Yuruk Semâî* (one). See Figure 17.

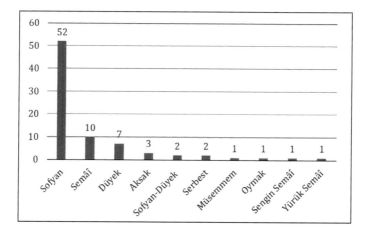

Figure 17: Usul Frequency of Use

TEXTS

The third component of Turgay's songs is the text. Having decoded the various aspects of the two major organizing principles of Turkish art music—the makam and usul systems—I had someone else complete the lyric translations, as I was not sufficiently fluent in the language.

Part Three: Praying Twice: Modes and Means

Translation Issues

Few Westerners are equipped to understand the subtleties of Turkish meta-phors in songs, as these are embedded in the Islamic culture of the society. Turgay is culturally a Muslim and spiritually a follower of Christ. He rejects Islam doctrinally but maintains his cultural identity. What does this mean? Turgay explains, "I'm now more comfortable as a disciple of Christ. I don't have a barrier with anyone, because I'm in the Muslim community. I'm still a Turk, inside the culture."[22]

As psychologist Chana Ullman notes, the identity of religious converts has elements of continuity with the past as well as discontinuity.[23] This viewpoint is shared by Rudolf Heredia,[24] who states, "They do not erase their former identity; rather, the new one is overwritten on it." It appears to be difficult to throw off the sense of belonging to the Muslim *ummah* (community) in terms of linguistic and cultural symbols.

In view of this phenomenon, two career missionaries fluent in Turk-ish spirituality translated the texts. Turgay, as the final authority, checked the song texts, infrequently making corrections or changing the translated meanings of his lyrics.

The Music-Making Process

What is Turgay's process of creating a song: lyrics, coherent melody, and rhythm?[25] For Turgay, there is not really a process. His songs come as a pack-age: music and words together in cultural form, as I described at the begin-ning of this chapter. They come to him in different situations and times. Some have happened while he was driving between Supanca—the family summer home—and Istanbul. Others occurred while he was shaving, riding public transportation, or engaging in solitary worship. He explains:

> I always stand or bow down [prostrate in the Middle Eastern con-text], hold my hands like this [palms turned upward], and I turn in different directions, because I am observing temple worship. Sometimes when I am reciting, it is like I am chanting the Bible

---

22. Üçal, interview, July 15, 2013.

23. Green, "Conversion in the Light of Identity Theories," loc. 1387.

24. Heredia, *Changing Gods: Rethinking Conversion in India*, 127.

25. I did not add the word *harmony*, because Turkish music is monophonic.

passages or psalms as I read them. Then the spontaneous music making of songs begins.[26]

Funda, Turgay's eldest daughter, corroborates Turgay's description. She remembers that when she was a child, her father liked to sing. "Whenever he was praying, songs were going on. He was praying, like singing a song."[27] Funda's description makes one think of the famous expression attributed to St. Augustine, "He who sings, prays twice."

One song came while Turgay was teaching a seminary class on Elijah. He remembers thinking, "What does it mean for my life?" A few weeks later, he started to sing:

Listen closely, O my heart, 'midst the sound of silence.

Not in the wind or the breeze, or the fire, or the flood.

Speak, speak to my heart with your sweet and soft voice.

Speak, O Word, speak to my heart; speak, deep down in my heart[28]

Turgay believes that his worship songs express a consciousness of God's love for Turkish citizens. He comments, "When they sing them, Turkish people are reminded of their six-hundred-year-old DNA!"[29]

Song Text Analysis

Next, I focus on six components of textual analysis. See Table 8 for my sample content analysis form. I supplemented this method with ethnographic material drawn from my thirty-two hour of interviews with Turgay in addition to his writings.

Table 8: Sample Content Analysis Form

Title	Trinity	Biblical Texts	Metaphors	God	Us	Function
Taht önünde o haşette (Before the Throne)	Father—3 Messiah—2 Spirit—1		Throne, glory; majesty; Light; you are there and so am I		Heaven	Proclamation
Duydum, duydum, duymadım (I Listened and Listen, but Never Understood)	Lord God—2	Matt 13:14—15	Darkness, the Light	Mercy		Exhortation

26. Üçal, interview, July 15, 2013.

27. Funda, interview, July 30, 2013.

28. Üçal, Song 31, from 1 Kgs 19, 11–12.

29. Üçal, interview, July 15, 2013.

BIBLICAL ANALYSIS

What can one learn about God from Turgay's indigenous hymnody, the Word in song? Thirty-three of his eighty songs focus on specific verses or chapters in the Bible. Twenty-two of them reference the Old Testament, and eleven reference the New Testament. The performance of these works in the ASM worship event and social history provides a contextualization of the Word in its natural culture and ethos.

For example, in Song 17 based on Psalm 25, Turgay confesses he has strayed from the ways of God. He begs God not to leave him in his shame:

> I draw near to you. I have strayed from your ways.
>
> Do not leave me in my shame, my Lord and my God.
>
> You are my Lord God, my King, and my Ruler.
>
> Teach me your paths. Give me your direction.
>
> Put to death my selfishness, my Lord and my God.[30]

This relates to Turkey's Eastern culture in its collectivism, group-orientation, and cultural values of honor and shame. Feeling guilty and humiliated, Turgay wants not only the removal of his guilt and condemnation from God, but also the covering of his shame before man and the restoration of his honor before God. See Figure 18 for the list of thirty-three scriptural references used in this study's collection of eighty songs.

---

30. Uçal, Song 17 in this study.

Genesis 1	Isaiah 42:8
Genesis 2:10	Isaiah 43:1–2
Numbers 6:24–27	Isaiah 44:6
Deuteronomy 6	Isaiah 49:16
I Chronicles 4	Matthew 5
I Chronicles 4:10	Matthew 7:7 and Isaiah 55:6
I Kings 19:11–12	Matthew 13:14–15
Psalm 18:6	John 1
Psalm 25	John 4:21
Psalm 51	John 14:5
Psalm 96:9	John 14:6
Psalm 100	John 19:17
Psalm 117	I John 1:5
Psalm 134 and 28:2	Ephesians 4:4–6
Psalm 143:6	Revelation 7:12
Isaiah 12:3	TOTAL: 33

Figure 18: Biblical References in Songs

Author Bruce Malina, author of *The New Testament World: Insights from Cultural Anthropology,* states, "The words we use to say and speak do in fact embody meaning, but the meaning does not come from the words. Meaning inevitably derives from the general social system of the speakers of the language."[31] Simply put, the cultural values of the civilizations we study in the Bible—including Asia Minor (Turkey)—are different from those of contemporary Christians in the West. Likewise, Turgay's song texts are different from those of contemporary Christians in the West. His cultural metaphors are rooted in the East.

METAPHORS

Among the many metaphors embedded in Turgay's works, one stands out from the others as an illustration of his background. The meaning can be easily understood by those inside the culture, but not by modern-day Western Christians. In Song 74 from Isa 44:6, Turgay sings the following:

> You are the first, O Lord; you are the last, O Lord.
>
> Nothing equals or resembles you.
>
> All things are the work of your hands.

31. Malina, *New Testament World,* 1–2.

You washed away my sin, looked me in the eye.

You filled me with the love that is in Christ.

The remarkable import of the fourth line—"You washed away my sin, looked me in the eye"—is lost on outsiders. Its meaning is related to the sultan's lofty position during the nearly six-hundred-year Ottoman Empire (1476–1923), when there was a huge chasm separating the sultan from his citizens. Because his status was so far above his subjects, it was forbidden for lowly citizens to look at him. They had to bow in his presence and hide their faces. With a nod to this historic fact, Turgay makes the point that God, the supreme sultan, is a different kind of sultan: "Nothing equals or resembles you. All things are the work of your hands." Contrary to the customs of Ottoman rulers, our Lord and Master invites us to gaze at his face as he looks us in the eye with mercy, grace, and love.

By concentrating on cultural texts, Turgay gives new voice to the Istanbul Christian community and provides understanding of the general culture from *inside* the culture. Robert Schreiter writes, "The poet has the task of capturing those symbols and metaphors which best give expression to the experience of a community."[32] With a caveat, he counsels, "The validity of poetic insight has to be tested on more than aesthetic criteria or resonance with a community's experience."[33] In the context of ASM, this validation must, of necessity, be tested at the global theological community level, since the majority of churches in Turkey are Western-oriented instead of Turkish.

THEMES

Turgay is very intentional in his use of theological terms, especially when it comes to the characteristics and names for God. See Table 9 for his ten most frequently used themes in the order of frequency. Out of the eighty songs analyzed, Lord and the Trinity concept in various combinations (Creator, Savior; the Word, Christ, Jesus, or Messiah; and Holy Spirit) are most frequently used. This terminology is reflected in Turgay's approach to liturgy and in his sermons as well. He is consistent in practice, because many Muslim background believers (MBBs) struggle with understanding the spiritual concepts of Jesus, the Son of God, and the triune God, the Trinity.

---

32. Schreiter, *Constructing Local Theologies*, 19.

33. Schreiter, *Constructing Local Theologies*, 19.

Table 9: Names for God, Themes, and Frequency

Names	Themes	Frequency
Lord	22	92
God	20	80
Trinity (three in one)	22	38
The Word	17	21
Christ/Savior/Jesus	14	33
Messiah	8	38
Light	6	11
Holy Spirit	5	44
Creator	4	18
Mastor	3	10
TOTAL: 10	121	385

Due to a considerable number of themes within some songs, the themes required further grouping into subcategories, as illustrated in Table 10. The topic of believers had the largest number of themes, but the topic of God occurred most frequently.[34]

Table 10: Song Topics, Themes, and Frequency

Topics	Themes	Frequency
Believers	23	13
God	22	92
Word	17	18
Christ/Savior/Jesus	14	29
Messiah	8	48
Holy Spirit	5	30
Light	5	11
Prayer	5	62
TOTAL: 8	99	303

As I compared the number of themes versus the number of songs, I noticed that there are ninety themes in eighty songs. That means 1.24 themes average per song. At first, it seemed like a low theme rate when compared to the high text load and multiple themes of Western hymns.

34. See Appendix I for final coverage of Turgay's lyric theology, including more song topics, themes, and frequency of use.

However, the low theme rate is directly related to the assembly's song form of choice, the *şarkı*. Because the *şarkı* has a couplet literary form (repetitive four-bar phrases), it is unable to carry a large text load.

I have since concluded that Turgay's 1.24 average theme-rate occurrence is normal for Turkey. Repetition, repetition, repetition is the key learning tool in his culture. The traditional learning techniques in oral cultures such as Turkey are purposed to receive, preserve, and transmit orally from one generation to another. Thus, I accept that ASM's low text load and theme rate is different from that observed in Western literary cultures. I view it positively through its cultural lens, for I see that Turgay supplements gaps or losses with verbally-communicated discipleship enrichment.

The last consideration for Turgay's anthology of hymns was to explore the songs' primary functions. While there are various liturgical function codes listed by Western authors such as Constance Cherry,[35] Nathan Corbitt,[36] and Donald Hustad,[37] I identified four categories of hymn texts based upon my survey of ASM's repertoire—praise, exhortation, supplication, and proclamation. See Figure 19.

What does this mean? First, the results show that the praise of God is highly valued at ASM, with forty-four songs out of the eighty consisting of praise. That number is a little more than half the assembly's repertoire. The other songs are instrumental in helping to teach and admonish one another in wisdom and with thankfulness in their hearts.

Song Functions	Frequency
Praise	44
Exhortation	17
Supplication	16
Proclamation	3
TOTAL: 4	TOTAL: 80

Figure 19: Song Functions and Frequency

Next, I did a word-based technique of counting repeated words, uncovering topics of importance to Turgay or to those who sing these songs.

35. Cherry, *Worship Architect*, 274–75.
36. Corbitt, *Sound of the Harvest: Music in Global Christianity*, 5.
37. Hustad, *Jubilate!*, 261–62.

Roy D'Andrade claims, "Perhaps the simplest and most direct indication of schematic organization in naturalistic discourse is the repetition of associative linkages."[38] I looked at what is frequently repeated and also at what is not present in the song texts in order to determine the basic theological beliefs being taught at ASM.

The results of this particular analysis show that Turgay's most frequent song function is praise. He proclaims the gospel through praise. He gives praise for the resurrected God,[39] who gives our hearts new life through Christ,[40] who saves through the Messiah, [41]who gave me living water and my thirst was satisfied,[42] who is the Lord and Master and the only one who can save me, [43]and on and on. In other words, the proclamation of God's salvation offered through Jesus Christ is strong. Similarly, other topical categories do not stand alone; Turgay blends supplication with praise, and exhortation with praise as well.

Some aspects of evaluation of song content are arbitrary. Depending upon the attitude of the evaluator at the moment, the results may be skewed unless there are guidelines for the evaluation process. What about missing words and themes? Among the words or themes currently missing in Turgay's song texts are (1) the blood of Jesus that saves us (2) the return of Christ, and (3) the last judgment and hell. Why? Addressing every theological concept through music currently is not a priority to Turgay. The focus of his songs is on who God is, praise, salvation, and how to live as faithful followers of Christ day by day. See Appendix I for final coverage of themes in Turgay's lyric theology: God, the Father (theology), God, the Son (Christology), God, the Holy Spirit (pneumatology), believers (anthropology), church (ecclesiology), heaven (eschatology), and church activities (prayers).

It is safe to say that eighty songs are not a sufficient quantity to touch on all theological concepts; however, Turgay's songs are important components of the spiritual formation process taking place within the ASM body of believers. As he makes more music, Turgay will potentially deal with other inspiring biblical passages or verses.

---

38. D'Andrade, *Development of Cognitive Anthropology*, 294.

39. Uçal, Song 8 in this study.

40. Uçal, Song 16 in this study.

41. Uçal, Song 23 in this study.

42. Uçal, Song 14 in this study.

43. Uçal, Song 70 in this study.

TRANSMISSION

ASM is the production and dissemination source of Turgay's songs for the 165 Protestant congregations/fellowships in Turkey. When a spontaneously inspired worship song comes to Turgay's mind—with both lyrics and melody intact—he attempts to capture it as quickly as possible with a cell phone recorder. He then passes the new composition to Sibel, his wife, who checks the music by ear to determine if any changes or reworking are needed. When deemed pleasing, it is introduced to congregants during the ASM worship event or during the Tuesday morning class meeting where Turgay observes the impact on the worshipers. What impactful indications does he look for?

Worshipers respond to music's effects in various ways. These responses can be emotional, spiritual, or aesthetic. Music making may evoke a sense of the presence of God, which is reflected through worshipers' closed eyes, tears, and raised hands as well as the percussive sounds of clapping and the praising of God. Turgay takes these responses into account in his interpretation of music in ritual events. The goal is to incorporate meaningful songs into the song cycle.

By appropriating several traditional music styles and simple rhythmic forms in the creation of new worship songs, Turgay creates a hospitable worship experience in which communal music making is pleasing in sound, familiar to the ear, and technically accessible. Turgay realizes that music making is inherently social and that the experience is a form of social bonding.

Moreover, he understands that music evokes values and emotions related to many spheres of life, affecting "how a community's sense of identity is mediated in the musical-ritual action, beyond the spiritual-emotional qualities perceived in musical communication."[44] Others agree that it is in meaningful worship events that participants discover who they are in Christ as believers in Turkey.[45] Music has the capacity to embody many different meanings due to its multifaceted forms of impact.

One inherent means of music transmission within the church in Turkey is the personal network. Congregants share the music with family and friends, some of whom visit the church to hear the intriguing music in a

44. McGann, *Exploring Music as Worship and Theology*, 27.

45. Jennings, "On Ritual Knowledge," 113. I refrain from using the term "Turkish" believers or "Turkish" Christians, as Turkey is a multicultural country of Kurds, Turks, Armenians, Syrians, and many others whose first source of identity is ethnicity.

live setting. That was my experience. I was touched when I heard Turgay's recorded songs in the US, and I made a point of visiting ASM after I moved to Istanbul in the summer of 2008.

This interest in Turgay's music making led me to become part of a transmission process, similar to the work of well-known ethnomusicologist Kay Kaufman Shelemay, who got involved with the music of Jews of Syrian descent.[46] Following my summer practicum[47] at ASM in 2008, I became a co-facilitator, gradually coming alongside Turgay to help transmit his songs.

Our first collaboration was the production of the *Hakır Yüreğim* CD album (Cry Out, My Heart) in 2014, a two-disc collection of fifteen songs featuring the voice of his wife, Sibel. One disc is in Turkish, and the other in English. The purpose was twofold: (1) to supply indigenous music resources for his own congregation and other Protestant fellowships, as well as (2) to encourage foreign church planters in launching culturally appropriate worship songs from the very beginning of their evangelistic activities.[48]

Music as Material Culture

The material forms of music at ASM include its one-of-a-kind prayer book, sheet music, and two musical instruments: a baby grand piano and a Turkish large-frame hand drum *(bendir)*. Instruments used within the church are circumscribed by Turgay's theology of worship, an approach that rules out any configuration of electronic instruments—drums, guitar, bass, or acoustic drum set. Turgay welcomes Turkish and European classical instruments, but currently, ASM is without musicians with those capabilities except for one violinist.

His vision is to have a church orchestra composed of both Western and Eastern instruments. This vision would require instrumentalists to read music in both Eastern and Western music systems.

SHEET MUSIC AND WORSHIP SONGBOOK

From 2004 through 2005, the concerted efforts of a short-term musical worker named Virginia Marion resulted in the transcription of Turgay's

46. Shelemay, *Ethnomusicologist*, 189–204.

47. A requirement for my master's degree in intercultural studies at Fuller Seminary (2011).

48. New "workers" (missionaries) generally have no comprehension of the local musical system and are unaware of where to find indigenous musical resources.

first twenty-five hymns in the Turkish makam music system. A spiral-bound booklet, *Sabbath Ritual and Hymns*, documents the initial stage of his musical productivity, signaling to those around him the first indications of a prolific composer. By the time his second publication, *Worship Hymns for the Messiah* (2012) was released, the number of Turgay's musical works had risen to sixty-two.

My last collaborative efforts with Turgay before moving back to the states in 2017 resulted in the publication of *Hymns for Worship* (2017), a collection of eighty-seven of his compositions. These hymnbooks of indigenous songs and chants are available from ASM, in addition to the English-language and Western chord-chart versions.

Turgay's completed works today exceed the one hundred mark. In the footsteps of Sibel's output of recordings, Turgay's worship songs have taken on a life of their own.

CD Albums and Music Videos

Together, Sibel and Turgay have produced seven CD albums. The first three CDs featured locally translated foreign songs. The last four contained works of Turgay that increased in number with each subsequent CD. See all six album covers in Appendix H.

Turgay's first recorded indigenous song was heard on a 2002 recording. It was followed by three albums—the latest in 2014. This musical accomplishment has not gone unnoticed in Turkey's public spaces, as evidenced by the recent book, *Müzik ve Kimlik* (Music and Identity),[49] by Professor Rıdvan Şentürk of Istanbul Commerce University. Şentürk includes Turgay in his interviews of twenty-three respected national composers of different religious perspectives who express their spiritual identity through Ottoman-Turkish music. Turgay's interview (in Turkish) is available on YouTube, along with ten recordings featuring the vocal artistry of Sibel.[50]

The process of writing and producing original musical materials in the Turkish makam style became critical to Turgay's early pastoral efforts after he left his first church. It was important to him to produce traditional music as a vehicle of inculturation for the growing community he shepherded. Thus, the third and fourth albums of twelve songs

49. Şentürk, "Turgay Üçal," 411–21.

50. See Turgay's YouTube interview in Turkish here: https://www.youtube.com/watch?v=uXmAyPAeAlY, and one of his songs performed by Sibel here: https://www.youtube.com/watch?v=5r21JYMwHNo

each followed in quick succession—*Almighty* (2004) and *Created to Give Glory* (2005). These were ultimately packaged under one title: *Hallelujah: Turkish Christian Hymns in the Sufi Tradition* (Appendix H). All songs are Turgay's compositions. The songs are performed by Sibel and accompanied by Turkish classical instruments.

On the seventh recording, *As a Parched Land Thirsts* (2008), Turgay contributed nine of the thirteen tracks. Turkish composers created two tracks, and two more are anonymous Middle Eastern worship songs. Still, the East-West distinctive musical styles continued to be represented, as illustrated in Sibel's next recording, *Approaching the Table* (2008). She drew inspiration from several sources: contemporary Christian music, traditional Turkish culture, new Turkish hybrid songs, and pan-Middle Eastern musical traditions.

Our next to the last collaborative project (completed in 2017), produced fifteen music videos based on the 2014 *Cry Out, My Heart* CD Turkish music and language soundtracks. They now air on Kanal Hayat, a Christian TV station in Turkey and YouTube.[51] Turgay's songs are accessible in both the Turkish and the Western music notational systems, as well as digital recording and music video formats.

The hymnody practice of the All Saints Moda church is a significant illustration of what Protestant ethnomusicologists Vida Chenoweth and Darlene Bee first noted: "When a people develops its own hymns with both vernacular words and music, it is good evidence that Christianity has truly taken root."[52] In essence, inculturation in Turkey is critical to bringing in a harvest of souls into the Kingdom of God.

SUMMARY

In this chapter, I analyzed different components of Turkey's music culture and aesthetics, including the following: makamlar (melodies), usul-s (rhythmic modes), text, style, genre, composition, and transmission. These elements function in the inculturated worship service of the ASM church community in ways that deeply touch the people's lives and enrich their worship.

Turgay has an understanding and commitment to the significance of local music and the arts that is rare among local pastors in Turkey. The 165

51. "Cry Out, My Heart" https://www.youtube.com/watch?v=gHThnmaIYnU&list= RDgHThnmaIYnU&start_radio=1&t=6.

52. Chenoweth and Bee, "On Ethnic Music," 212.

local fellowships and approximately 1000 workers in the country (at last count in 2019) must be part of the solution, and not the problem. They must pick up the mantle of responsibility to encourage, empower, and support the development of indigenous worship arts in the church in Turkey.

The opportunities for evangelization are limitless. Turkey's eighty-three million citizens include the repressed Kurdish people group (20 percent of the population), and over three million Arabic-speaking refugees who languish in rural camps and city streets searching for a place to call home in the cultural milieu known as Turkey. Christians in this country have a God-ordained opportunity to impact the world for Christ.

8

A Model of Inculturation

THIS CHAPTER PRESENTS THE final results of my research. What is the outcome from my case study of a Turkish musical insider? What is its significance for the developing Protestant Church in Turkey? What are the implications for future research? But first, a look back at how we arrived here.

BACKGROUND

Two missional practitioners/scholars paved the way for this study: Roberta King in Côte d'Ivoire, with her four-arena matrix for studies in global church music, and Lila Balisky in Ethiopia, with her study of a pastor/composer. They verify the power of local Christian musicking to effectively communication the Gospel in ways that the spoken word cannot. While King's dissertation traces the development of Senufo-style hymnody in Africa by Senufo Christians, Balisky's dissertation sheds light on the life and ministry of a prolific composer/singer, Tesfaye Gabbiso, and his contribution to indigenous song in his home country and the wider world.[1]

Two additional works provided good progress along related lines of inquiry into the needs of MBBs. Careful to note that his work represents a start, theologian Mike Brislen's article describes "A Model for a Muslim-Culture Church." He writes,

1. See King, "Pathways in Christian Music Communication"; and Balisky, "Songs of Ethiopia's Tesfaye Gabbiso." Both of these dissertations have been published in the same series as the present monograph, the American Society of Missiology Monograph Series. See King, *Pathways in Christian Music Communication*; and Balisky, *Songs of Ethiopia's Tesfaye Gabbiso*.

Part Three: Praying Twice: Modes and Means

> A church consisting of believers out of a Muslim background must be contextualized into the local Islamic context. This contextualization must reach deeper than simply adapted worship forms; it must touch emotional, psychological, and theological levels of worldview. The needs of believers must be met by the church in this context of Muslim culture. The church must worship, express community, and witness to the kingdom of God in a Muslim context.[2]

Ruth Nicholls narrows down the topic in her dissertation, "Catechisms and Chants: A Case for using Liturgies in Ministry to Muslims":

> Theoretically, a possible solution to the problem of fostering Muslim seekers' spiritual growth was to develop culturally relevant and purpose focused liturgies. These liturgies, while reflecting Islamic culture, express Christian truths. Given that the Islamic salat reflects both the Jewish prayer cycle and the monastic daily office, the ritual form of the Daily Service of the Anglican tradition was chosen as the structural model. Having noted the principles relating to theology, culture, identification, language and flexibility, the next step is an example or model (2008, Abstract).[3]

In these investigations, cultural authenticity is a key value in ministry. Why? We need an interior sense of belonging. When we feel at home, we sense a deeper spiritual connection. We feel accepted, understood, and loved. Pastor Turgay Üçal has joined indigenous musicking and liturgy together—the first Protestant pastor in Turkey to do so.

COMING FULL CIRCLE

In this study, I evaluated the missional context, music maker, faith community, and biblical text to fathom the full scope of inculturation at All Saints Moda (ASM) in Istanbul, Turkey. My interdisciplinary exploration of ASM's worship event and the influence of Turgay's worship songs on the people were fleshed out through an array of methods drawn from theorists in liturgical studies, ethnomusicology, ritual studies, theology, and anthropology.

---

2. Brislen, "Model for a Muslim-Culture Church," 353–67.
3. Nicholls, "Catechisms and Chants . . .," ii.

152

Music Makers (Turgay Üçal's Spiritual Journey)

My attention in this arena focuses on the important events and influences in Turgay's life that led to the inception of musico-liturgical inculturation. What I learned about this aspect of his life was relatively simple: he needed to feel at home in worship, indicating the deepest level in the human mind and soul. Turgay now senses he has reached that place where he can be himself—culturally a Muslim and spiritually a Christ follower. It took him decades to reach this point.

Because of the nature of Christian worship, Turgay critically evaluated elements of Muslim culture before incorporating them into his communication, both linguistically, musically, and spiritually. When sharing the truth of the gospel, he has avoided leaning to the right or the left of the razor's edge, otherwise known as "obscurantism and syncretism,"[4] realizing the importance of inculturation for the church that wants to engage in God's mission.

Nevertheless, some leaders have falsely accused Turgay of a syncretic approach to Christianity. Those who know him best know he walks a fine line between the two issues. Like other committed church leaders who have gone before him, Turgay believes that elements of culture that cannot be made to harmonize with the practice of Christian faith must be left out.

Turgay sees himself theologically in step with the World Evangelical Alliance (WEA) and with the conservative Presbyterian camp as well. His statements of Reformed theology are found in ASM's prayer book[5] and include liturgical creedal statements like the first century Confession of Faith,[6] the Lord's Prayer,[7] and scriptural passages of the Lord's Table from the books of Mark and Luke.

Faith Community (All Saints Moda)

In this dimension, I looked into the role of music in ASM's worship event. Evoking the divine presence of God, local music, and other worship arts

4. Stetzer, "Avoiding the Pitfall of Syncretism," line 1. *Obscurantism* may be defined as blurring the gospel by using things that are outside the gospel as being central to it. *Syncretism*, on the other hand, is the mixing of Christianity with something unscriptural in a way that compromises the message. In each case, the practice leads to the creation of a false gospel.

5. Üçal, ASM prayerbook, 9, 11, 12, and 15.

6. 1 Tim 3:16.

7. Matt 6:9–13.

have shaped ASM's liturgy and theology. Worship is a living encounter—a powerful means of interacting with God through his Spirit, as participants sing praise, supplicate, exhort, and proclaim in combination with listening to his voice.

Music making at ASM allows songs to impact the aural character of the liturgy, reflecting cultural resonances and style of the church community. Faith and culture are inseparable. The congregants feel at home: the sounds within the church reflect the sounds of Istanbul, instead of a foreign culture.

Whereas inculturation generally is jointly implemented by people who represent different cultures, some church leaders like Turgay believe that the final step of inculturation can only be the work of those within the evangelized culture. This belief is affirmed in my investigation, which I outlined in chapters 5 through 7. The research data shows that Turgay's experimentations as an insider led to fruitful music-culture practices and procedures in ASM's communication of the gospel.

Biblical Text (Worship Songs)

Content and metaphor analyses of Turgay's song texts show solid biblical theology. Because it is impossible to cover every aspect of theology through ASM songs, Sunday sermons and various Bible studies throughout the week help fill the gaps.

RESULTS OF CARD SORTING—HYMN TITLES

Data collection through card sorting among eighteen ASM congregants indicates that although two preferred to sing indigenous hymns only and three preferred to sing translated Western hymns only, all indicated the belief that each of the nineteen music samples selected from their repertoire was appropriate for expressing authentic worship. Similarly, they set aside their preferences and worshiped with each song form, both local and foreign, for the sake of unity. See Appendix J.

RESULTS OF THE SURVEY—PARTICIPANTS

This research data corroborates the influence and efficacy of indigenous song, as shown in the longevity of Christian faith and the ongoing spiritual formation in twelve of the eighteen participants. See the last two columns in Table 11. Two-thirds of the people accepted Christ through the ministry of ASM. At the time of the research, four were relatively young in the faith (three years or less), and the others had been believers for four to twenty-plus years.

Table 11: Impact of Indigenous Hymnody on Participants

Gender	Age	Religious Background	Ethnicity	Length of time as a Believer	Length of time at ASM
M—4	20s—3	Sunni Muslim —8	Turks—9	3 yrs or less— 4	3 yrs or less—6
F—14	30s—4	Armenian Ortho—5	Armenians—6	4-10 yrs—3	4-10 yrs—3
	40s—7	Alevi—2	Kurds—2	11-20 yrs—5	11-20 yrs—9
	50s—3	Russian Ortho—2	Russian—1	over 20 yrs—1	
	60s—1	Protestant—1		Since childhood—5	

The last two distinguishing characteristics are unusual for churches in Turkey. In a country where nine out of ten who profess Christ as Savior leave the church within two years of conversion, the opposite was true at ASM. Twelve of the eighteen people in this investigation became Christ followers after visiting the church community and were still very much involved up to twenty years later.

My research shows that Turgay's indigenous music communicates with local people emotionally, cognitively, and behaviorally in powerful ways. They are open to the message of the song texts, and are growing spiritually due to the songs' formative ability to shape theology and influence their decision-making processes. ASM's hymnody functions like the Word of God in participants' lives, and become indicators of their beliefs, understandings, and actions, because the attitude toward the musical sound and song text is positive, not negative. Likewise, it fosters a sense of spiritual home and cultural belonging. See additional sample responses of these participants in Appendix K.

Missional Context (Istanbul, Turkey)

Istanbul is the cultural beginning and end of this study. It serves as the backdrop for ASM. While globalization has fractured the city's modern daily life, it has heightened its local sensibilities. More and more people are expressing their differences or uniqueness. The "we are, therefore I am" attitude of Istanbul's non-Western collectivists toward identity remains important to the people's culture. Traditional music is an essential component of the people's major passages of life. Correspondingly, Turkey's indigenous religious music has changed much more slowly than its popular music.

The challenge of bridging the gap between Christian faith and Eastern culture, however, is fundamentally unmet by missionaries and national church leaders. The Protestant church community in Turkey has yet to engage the local culture in a meaningful way, although it is experiencing growth in the area of worship. Along with the songs continuing to be translated from English into Turkish, a fair amount of original music (composed in Western styles) has been written and accepted by the church. These have grown out of youth camp ministries, conferences, and nationwide events that have influenced worship in the church.

Then again, though ASM's worldview differs significantly from its surrounding Islamic society, members enjoy a respected place in its setting and members function as leaders. Converts are open about their faith, sharing Christ through family connections and friendship evangelism. They are content in supporting and identifying with the way the contextualized church is structured.

IMPLICATIONS FOR INCULTURATION

Inculturation is an essential part of the outreach task of the church as believers know it to be: to share Christ and make him understood by people of a given culture, locality, and time. Music offers tangible ways of working *with* culture on God's behalf, instead of against or in ignorance of it. What steps might be considered by church leaders in Turkey for making the gospel in song at home in a local cultural context? I propose the following strategies.

Access the Church's Diverse Leadership

The Protestant church must be deliberate about gathering insight from those who typify the church's diversity, lest worship loses its relevance to the people's direct, firsthand experience of worship. My case study of Pastor Turgay Üçal's life and musico-liturgical inculturation demonstrates the potential fruitfulness of such incorporation. A more inclusive approach to missiological strategizing would produce better missiology and more authentic worship practices. This viewpoint leads to the next strategy: experimentation.

Experimentation

Musicians today must be encouraged at the local level to experiment with inculturation and must be allowed to incorporate results of successful experiments. They need freedom to interact with the cultures and religious values of surrounding people groups. It is not enough to present the gospel in the vernacular language, understood in only a literal sense. The gospel must be communicated to all peoples in all places, creatively retold and expressed through symbols already functioning in the predominant culture. This must continue into succeeding generations.

FUTURE DIRECTIONS

Like all studies, this one has weaknesses and limitations. However, it brings more questions to light and reveals more areas of interest to pursue outside the scope of this research. I am hopeful that someone will continue to pursue an understanding of those topics having to do with the local worship practices discussed and move the conversation forward. Will church leaders incorporate collaborative efforts with imagination and vision?

Who will initiate intervention among young musicians through music conferences and song-writing workshops where worship interpretations are reframed, vision is cast, and experimentation is urged? Local music makers must challenge the next generation to create solid theological songs in indigenous styles. Further, who will build upon the nationwide efforts of the Turkish government to safeguard and promote its own musical culture among the youth?

In 2006, the music education system in Turkey introduced a common music repertoire into the music training classes at the primary and junior high school levels throughout the country. This Turkish repertoire is strategically meant to sustain the music of the people, reinforcing and developing Turkish unity and solidarity by ensuring national tunes are strong and more familiar than foreign tunes, while at the same time maintaining respect for others on the global stage. Those are admirable goals.

Bearing in mind that the youth represent the church of tomorrow, leaders would do well to consider that recent changes to Turkey's national school music curriculum provide an opening for initiating musico-inculturation. May such an eventuality contribute to supplementing the Western approach to Christian worship in Turkey and result in a vast spiritual harvest. What are you prepared to do about it?

ASM—A Model of Inculturation

I pray that the inculturation process Turgay has pioneered will catch fire. I envision that the upcoming generation of church leaders will grasp the vision to create opportunities for believers from a Muslim background and others like them to identify with local expressions of culture and community. May they preserve a dynamic allegiance to Christ and kingdom work, and feel at home in worship, while fostering Christlike identity and spiritual formation.

Appendix A

Üçal Publications and Papers

İbadet İlahileri	İstanbul: GDK, 2012	Turkish Hymnal, 75 original hymns
Vakit İbadeti	Istanbul: GDK, 2012	Common Prayer Book
Yaratanı Yaşamak	İstanbul: GDK Yayınevi, 2012.	Study on Luke
Efendimiz Buyuruyor ki	İstanbul: GDK Yayınevi, 2012.	Study on Matthew
Kilise	İstanbul: GDK Yayınevi, 2012.	Study on Acts
İman Edinimi	İstanbul GDK, 2010	Study on Romans
Kahinlik Seviyesi	İstanbul GDK, 2010	Study on Leviticus
İhsan Eden Rab	İstanbul GDK, 2009	Study on İsaiah
Çöl Tecrübesi	İstanbul GDK, 2009	Study on Exodus
Önderlik	İstanbul: Haberci, 2006	Study on Pastoral Leadership
Kilise Minberinden	İstanbul: Gerçeğe Doğru, 2005	Sermons
Misyonerlik	İstanbul: Gerçeğe Doğru, 2002	To be a Missionary
Günlük İbadet	İstanbul: Anadolu Ofset, 2001	Daily Worship
Anadoluya Sesleniş	İstanbul: Gerçeğe Doğru, 2001	Study on Revelation
Hrisitiyan Ahları	İstanbul: Öb Asta, 2000	Ethics
Pastörün Seyir Defteri	İstanbul: Asya, 2000	Articles on Faith

Appendix A: Üçal Publications and Papers

Yakup James	İstanbul: Ön Asya, 2000	Study on epistle of
Tanrı Çizgisi	İstanbul: Kaya Yayıncılık, 1998	God's Line—Sharing Christ with Turks
Damla Damla Christian Radio	İstanbul: Müjde Yayıncılı, 1995	Evangelistic Poems for
Mesihle Yaşamak Does it Mean	İstanbul: Müjde Yayıncılık, 1994	Life with Christ: What
	İstanbul: Müjde Yayıncılık, 1999	3rd Printing

Languages

Turkish: Native language
English: Speaks, reads and writes fluently
Persian: Reads fluently, speaks
Arabic: Reads
Ottoman Turkish: Reads

Appendix B

Photographs

Photo 1: Turgay leading worship with *bendir*

Appendix B: Photographs

Photo 2: Preaching

Photo 3: Üçal family

Photo 4: Recent Christmas Eve Outreach Service (inside)

Photo 5: Same Christmas Eve Service (outside)

Appendix C

Schedule of Interviews and Follow-Up Question/Answer Emails with Turgay

Date	Length - Hr	Minutes	Location
7/8/13	1	49.8	ASM Church Office
7/15/13	2	22	ASM Church Office
7/30/13	0	49.9	Historic Home in Mudanya
8/26/13	1	43.6	ASM Church Office
9/1/13	1	60.6	ASM Church Office
9/22/13	1	57.5	ASM Church Office
10/22/13	1	36.5	ASM Church Office
10/23/13	1	22.3	ASM Church Office
11/18/13	1	17.5	ASM Church Office
11/20/13	1	34.2	ASM Church Office
11/26/13	1	34.1	ASM Church Office
1/21/14	1	44.0	ASM Church Office
2/4/14	1	21.5	ASM Church Office
3/11/14	1	39.5	ASM Church Office
9/9/14	1	13.5	ASM Church Office
1/4/15	1	27.4	ASM Church Office
2/9/15	1	0.4	ASM Church Office
2/25/15	1	28.5	ASM Church Office
5/25/15	0	36.1	ASM Church Office
6/10/15	1	6	ASM Church Office
10/19/15	1	24.4	ASM Church Office
3/21/16	0	4.6	ASM Church Office
5/4/16	0	38	ASM Church Office
6/21/16	0	10.5	ASM Church Office

Total Time: 32 hrs, 2.4 min

QUESTION/ANSWER EMAILS

Sue	Turgay
7/30/14	7/30/14
7/30/14	7/31/14
9/28/14	9/29/14
12/6/14	12/6/14
1/27/15	1/30/15
2/16/15	2/17/15

Sue	Turgay
3/5/15	3/5/15
6/2/15	6/3/15
6/29/16	6/30/16
7/1/16	7/1/16
7/13/16	7/13/16

Appendix D

Other Communications

PASTORS OF THE LARGEST PROTESTANT CHURCHES IN ISTANBUL[1]

Carlos Madrigal, interview, Istanbul Protestant Church, Istanbul, November 11, 2013.

Kırkor Ağabaloğ, interview, Gedikpaşa New Testament Church [Armenian], Istanbul, September 23, 2013.

Levent Kımran, interview, Starbucks in Kadiköy (Istanbul), November 16, 2015.

MINISTRY LEADERS IN TURKEY

C. H., email exchange, 2014–2015.

D. H., interview, restaurant, Kadiköy (Istanbul), June 19, 2015.

David Phillips, email exchange, May 5, 2016 and May 7, 2016.

G. C., email exchange, June 10, 2013 and June 12, 2013.

Ilhan Keskinöz, interview, restaurant, Kadiköy (Istanbul), August 7, 2016.

O. J., interview, coffee shop, Kadiköy (Istanbul), July 25, 2013.

Reşit Başaran, email exchange, November 17, 2015 and December 6, 2015.

Scott and Christine DeVries, Skype, August 4, 2016.

WORSHIP LEADERS IN TURKEY

Aaron, Starbucks, Kadiköy (Istanbul), November 25, 2014.

    1. Turgay Üçal is in this group.

Andy, SIL office, Kadiköy (Istanbul), November 25, 2014.

Erman, St. Paul's Center, Antalya, November 23, 2014.

G. M., St. Paul's Center, Antalya, November 24, 2014.

Gürkan, *Yeni Yaşam Yayınları*, Istanbul, October 7, 2013.

Jessica, SIL office, Kadiköy (Istanbul), November 25, 2014.

Julian, St. Paul's Center, Antalya, November 24, 2014.

Metin, St. Paul's Center, Antalya, November 22, 2014.

Ögül, restaurant, Besiktaş (Istanbul), November 26, 2014.

Steve, SIL office, Kadiköy (Istanbul), November 25, 2014.

V. V., SIL office, Kadiköy (Istanbul), November 25, 2014.

FAMILY AND FRIENDS

David H., restaurant, Kadiköy (Istanbul), June 15, 2015.

Funda, interview, historic home, Mudanya, July 30, 2013.

G. C., interview, historic home, Mudanya, July 30, 2013.

O. J., interview, Starbucks, Kadiköy (Istanbul), November 13, 2014.

Sibel, interview, Üçal apartment, Istanbul, June 13, 2013.

TURGAY ÜÇAL IN ARTICLES, BLOGS, DISSERTATION, AND BOOK

Bultema, James. "Muslims Coming to Christ in Turkey." *International Journal of Frontier Missiology* 27 (2010) 27–31.

Carnes, Tony. 2008. "Jesus in Turkey." In *Christianity Today*, January 3, 2008.

Coachbunch. 2013. "Experiencing Turkey in 2013." *The Bunch Real Estate Group* (blog), October 15, 2013. http://coachbunch.com/tag/all-saints-moda.

Hogaboam, Rick. 2008. "Emotional Calvinism Reaching Muslims in Turkey." *Endued* (blog), March 21, 2008. https://endued.wordpress.com/tag/turgay-ucal/.

Pikkert, "Protestant Missionaries to the Middle East: Ambassadors of Christ or Culture?" PhD diss., Pretoria, South Africa: University of South Africa, 2006, 272.

Şentürk, Rıdvan. "Turgay Üçal." In *Müzik Kimlik*, 411–21. Istanbul: Küre Yayınları, 2016.

Wade, Chris. "A Small Piece of Turkish Christianity." *Digital Journal*, June 20, 2001. http://www.digitaljournal.com/article/32879.

Wallace, Cory, ed. "Devastation in Turkey: The Church Responds." *Mission Frontiers*, Jan 1, 2000.

Appendix E

A Turgay Hymn in Two Music Systems and Languages

20. Hymn in the Turkish Music System and Language

21. Hymn in the Western Music System and English

Appendix F

ASM Prayer Book Cover with Sample Ottoman Artwork

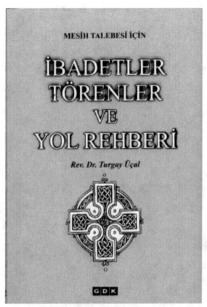

This easy-to-carry book is a contextualized resource, giving prominence to the Sunday liturgy along with special days and occasions, including scriptural readings and prayers for each day of the year. It also contains the current collection of texts for 107 of Turgay Üçal's songs and chants. The prayer books are a mainstay on the back of the All Saints Moda pews for use in the liturgy and are free for the taking.[1]

---

1. Valued by a cross-section of followers of Christ—including those inside and outside the local assembly, Turkey, and the broader world—Turgay's prayer books (in Turkish) are also available in the church office.

Appendix G

ASM Ten-Week Cycle of Hymns (2013)

Week	Ten Weeks of Worship Songs				
1	B *Hayatım Sende, Rab!* My Life is in you, Lord! (IH)	B *Çağınnıml Merhamet elini uzat bana!* Good to Me (V)	B *Tüm gökyüzü* All Heav'n Declares (M)	C *Dinle yüreğim dinle**** Listen Closely, O My Heart	C *Korkma, korkma* Fear Not, Fear Not
2	A *Hamdim Sana**** My praise is to You	B *İşte Ruh ve gelin* Here's what the Spirit and the Bride say, "Come!" (Canadian)	B *utsallığına baktığımda* When I Look into Your Holiness (IH)	C *Yükselt sesin yer* Raise Your Voice, Earth	C *Bir iman, bir vaftiz**** One Faith, One Baptism
3	B *Ruhun içi doldursun!* May Your Spirit Fill Me/ The Name of the Lord/What a Mighty God	B *Rab, ne ulussun!* Great is the Lord (K. Prosch, MV)	B *Eğer göklere çıksam Sen ya Rab* If I Ascend to the Heavens, You are There	C *Ey Şanı yüce Olan* O, You Glorious One	C *Ey Yaratan, lütfet bana**** O Creator, Please Have Mercy
4	B *Hosanna, hosanna* Hosanna, Hosanna (MV)	A *Ey Yaratan, layıksın Sen* O Creator, You are Worthy	A *Yaşadığım sürece* As Long as I Shall Live	C *Haykır yüreğim**** Cry Out, My Heart	A *Gözlerimi dağlara kaldırıyorum* I Raise My Eyes to the Mountains
5	A *Rabbe şükretmek**** Giving Thanks to the Lord	B *O Rabbimizdir ve gökten seslenir* He is the Lord, and He Reigns on High (MV)	B *Senin sevgin ömürden güzeldir* Your Lovingkindness (Straightway Music)	C *Dünya denen bu çölde**** In this Desert Called the World	C *Ben Sana geldim aşk ile**** I Have Come to You with Love
6	B *Rabbin sarsılmaz**** The Steadfast Love (Celebration)	B *Senin sevgin ömürden güzeldir* Your Lovingkindness (Straightway Music)	B *İsmin üstündür**** You Have been Given a Name Above All Names (Sovereign Grace)	C *Büküktü belim dokundu* My back was Bent Over, Your Hand Touched It	C *Duydum duydum duymadım**** I Listened and Listened, But Never Understood
7	B *Halleluya, kadir olan* Hallelujah, for the Lord our God (UMP, N.Z.)	B *Seni yüçeltiniz* We are Here to Praise You (GK-U.K.)	B *Bir hayat suyu akandır* Shall We Gather at the River (traditional)	C *Ey Yaratan, ey ışık* O Creator, O Light	C *Dilim Sana övgü söyler**** My Tongue praises You
8	B *Kutlayacağım Rabbimizi* I Will Celebrate (Hosanna)	B *Halkın arasıda Sana* Be Exalted (Integrity)	B *Tanrım derim, güvenirim**** I Call you My God, I Trust you	C *Benliğimden kopan fırtına* Storms Within Me	C *Yürek "bana" doğrudur* My heart is all about "Me"
9	B *Budur Rabbin**** This is the Day (Integrity)	B *Sen, ya Rab* You, O Lord, Rich in Mercy (EMI, U.K.)	B *Baba senin sevgin**** Father God, I Wonder (EMI, U.K.)	C *Yüreğimdeki o yarış* That Burning in my heart	C *Kurtuluş pınarlarına vardım**** I Came to the Springs of Salvation
10	B *Kutsal, kutsal, kutsal Rabdir* Holy, Holy, Holy is the Lord of Hosts (M)	B *Şükret içtenlikle* Give Thanks (IH)	B *Daha sevgi, daha güç**** More Love, More Power (Vineyard)	C *Kurak toprak gibi**** As Parched Land Thirsts	C *Kaldır Perdeyi göster* Lift the Veil, Display the Truth

172

Appendix G: ASM Ten-Week Cycle of Hymns (2013)

Key: Hymns used in the card-sorting interviews are marked with three asterisks

A = Turkish folksong style (5)

B = Translated Western (26)

C = Turkish *Sanat*-Sufi style (19)

173

Appendix H

CD Albums of ASM Worship Songs (1998–2014)

Photo 7: *Donün Rab Binize*
(Return to Your Lord)
Sibel Üçal, soloist (1998)

Appendix H: CD Albums of ASM Worship Songs (1998–2014)

Photo 8: *Halleluya: İsevi-Sufi Geleneği Hristiyan Türk İlahileri*
(Hallelujah: Turkish Christian Hymns in the Sufi Tradition)
Sibel Üçal, soloist (2001–2002), double disc

Photo 9: *Varlığının Sakinliğinde*
(In the Calm of His Presence)
Sibel Üçal, soloist (2002)

Photo 10: *Kurak Toprak Gibi*

(As a Parched Land Thirsts)

Sibel Üçal, soloist (2007)

Photo 11: *Sofraya Yaklasırken*

(Approaching the Table)

Sibel Üçal, soloist (2008)

Photo 12: *Haykır Yüreğim*

(Cry Out, My Heart)

Sibel Üçal, soloist (2014)

Appendix I

Lyric Theology

Topic: God (theology)

Themes	Frequency
Teaches/directs	20
On throne in heaven	19
Gives new life	18
First and the Last	17
Faithful	16
Unchanging	15
Kindness/goodness	13
Powerful	12
Peace	11
Protects/helps/shelters	10
Holy	9
Purifies/cleanses/restores	8
One God/Father, Son and Holy Spirit	7
Blesses	6
Eternal	5
Cures/heals	4
Merciful/sufficient grace	4
Loves	3
Saves/forgives/redeems/delivers/pardons	2
Worth of our praise	1
Total Items: 20	200

Figure 20: God (theology)

Topic: God, the Son (Christology)

Themes	Frequency
Messiah	26
Forgives	19
The Word/Truth	18
Delivers/heals/renews	11
Walks with me/talks with me	11
Peace	10
Suffered and died for us/Savior/won the victory over death	10
Loves us	9
The way/the way to heaven	8
Salvation/saves	7
Worthy of our praise	6
Transforms/gives new live	5
Calls/cleanses	4
Lives/resurrection life/resurrected	2
Shelters	1
Total Items: 15	147

Figure 21: God, the Son (Christology)

Topic: God, the Holy Spirit (pneumatology)

Themes	Frequency
Makes us one	12
Lives within us	12
Transforms us	5
Guides/directs/helps	3
Sent by God	3
Total:5	35

Figure 22: God, the Holy Spirit (pneumatology)

Appendix I: Lyric Theology

Topic: Believers (anthropology)

Themes	Frequency
Worship and praise	28
Have new life through Christ / Have found the Way, Go to the Way, Believe Jesus Christ is the only way / Have been lifted out of darkness, Sins are washed away / Have Jesus is in their heart	9
Draw near / Come to God	9
Lift hands / Raise voices / Celebrate the Savior	8
Live eternally	7
Repent / Renounce and put away sin	6
Love God / Must know and love God	5
Saved / Transformed	4
Yearn, thirst /Hunger for God / Seek, search / Burn in their hearts for him	4
Bow down	4
Cry out / Call to God	4
Walk with God	4
Plead for mercy	3
People of God / Followers of God	2
Believe in the Trinity: Father, Son and Holy Spirit / Believe in one God	2
Happy being with God / Heart is empty without God	2
Are one in the Father, Son and Spirit	1
Believe in one baptism	1
Often seek in the wrong place. Must turn from problems to God's presence	1
Are at peace, filled with his Spirit	1
Listen closely to the voice of God	1
Find grace, find the Light	1
Soul is satisfied in Jesus, the Messiah	1
TOTAL: 23	108

Figure 23: Believers (anthropology)

Topic: Church (ecclesiology)

Themes	Frequency
Glorify and exalt the Lord	6
People of God, followers of God	2
Let's go to the Way	1
We must know and love God	1
Let us return to our Lord and repent	1
TOTAL: 5	11

Figure 24: Church (ecclesiology)

Topic: Heaven (eschatology)

Theme	Frequency
Before the Throne in that Glory	7
TOTAL	7

Figure 25: Heaven (eschatology)

Topic: Body of Christ (activities)

Theme	Frequency
Prayers	62
TOTAL	62

Figure 26: Body of Christ (activities)

Appendix J

Card-Sorting Procedures

This appendix describes the first step in my two-part research process of gathering responses from ASM participants about the music of Turgay Üçal. Interviews were conducted at the church during 2013 and 2014.

PROTOCOL AND SUBJECT IDENTITIES

After the introductions,[1] I briefly described my investigation of ASM's worship music and the importance of their participation in it. I requested that each subject sign the informed consent form and fill in the form for gathering basic personal information. This included the following: (1) gender, (2) age, (3) religious background, (4) ethnicity, (5) length of time as a believer, and (6) length of time at ASM. Bernard affirms that most survey researchers prefer close-ended items to open-ended questions, but he balances that out by saying, "People are apparently least threatened when they can offer their own answers to open-ended questions on a self-administered questionnaire"[2]

CARD-SORTING GUIDE AND RESPONSES

Explanation of my goals for the research:

1. Jaklin, Turgay's office assistant, and Sibel, his wife, both took responsibility for introducing me to the respondents as a way of giving the church's approval to the research that I undertook within the ASM assembly.

2. Bernard, *Social Research Methods*, 240.

- To learn from the participants how they mentally classify the hymns in their worship practice, what terms they use for the hymns, and how they feel about them.

- There are no wrong answers; all answers are correct.

- I will be recording the interviews so I can remember what was said. I will take photos of the card selections.

First, I handed the participants the nineteen cards of hymn titles regularly sung at ASM, then gave the following instructions:

> *I have given you nineteen cards with familiar hymn titles selected from the hymns sung here at the church. Please separate the cards into groups of your choosing. I am asking you to put songs that are similar together and to create a category name for each group. There are no right or wrong answers.*

When they completed the task, I asked the eighteen respondents to reveal their method of classification. See compiled responses of subjects below. I spent some time probing the reasons for their choices. It was important to allow respondents to describe in their own language and in their own categories of understanding why they chose their selections. Most subjects separated the songs into either three or four groups. One made two, and another made five. Seven of the eighteen interviews were conducted in English. The other eleven were translated by bilingual workers or congregants.

As indicated, there was a substantial consensus among the diverse respondents. All eighteen indicated their belief that the All Saints Moda's three song genres were culturally appropriate for use in the worship event. They laid aside their preferences for the sake of unity among the ASM body of believers, enthusiastically singing them all.

Table 12: Card-Sorting Compiled Responses

Attitude toward ASM Worship Songs	Respondents - o	Respondents - x
The Three Genres Deemed Approprate for Christian Communication	18	
Translated Western (TW) = o	16	
Translated Western (TW) = x		2
Turgay's songs (TMM) = o	15	
Turgay's songs (TMM) = x		3
Turkish folk songs (TF) = o	18	
Turkish folk songs (TF) = x		0

Key:
Preferred songs = o
Did not prefer = x

Two participants did not prefer translated Western (TW), and three did not prefer Turkish makam music (TMM). The two respondents who did not prefer TW were Turkish nationals who loved Üçal's worship songs. Of the three respondents who did not prefer TMM, the first one, a native Iranian, said, "I feel like a Muslim when I sing them." The second respondent, who had been raised in an evangelical church in Istanbul, had only sung TW. It was her heart music. The third person was a classically-trained pianist from Kazakhstan. Understandably then, that was *her* heart music.

No respondents indicated a "did not prefer" for Turkish folk songs (TF). Singing one TF per Sunday did not present a problem for any participant. Because TF is closer in style to TW, it appealed to the three respondents who preferred TW, and because TF was Turkish, the two respondents who preferred Turgay's songs also liked the TF because they are Turkish style.

Lastly, I said,

> *Thank you, this is the end. Is there anything else you would like to add to our discussion about the songs of ASM?* There was nothing added.

Appendix K

Survey Question Guide and Response Samples

This appendix encompasses an adaptation of King's interview question guide from her 1989 dissertation[1] for this investigation. The appendix also includes the sample hymn texts and responses from the interviews I conducted from 2013 to 2015.

SURVEY QUESTION GUIDE

Explanation of my goals:

a. To learn from the participants what they feel about the hymns.

b. There are no wrong answers; all answers are correct.

c. I will record the interview so I can remember what was said.

I handed the participants a list of the nine indigenous hymns from the semi-structured interviews (pile-sorting). I then asked the following questions.

Section I: Thoughts About the Indigenous-Style Hymns: Christ Followers

1. Which hymn touches you the most? Why? How?

2. Which hymns are meaningful to you? Do you have a specific story to tell about how these hymns have helped you?

1. King, "Pathways," 354–57.

3. Are there other hymns that have helped you in your Christian life? Which hymns are they? Can you tell us about them?

Section II. Thoughts about the Indigenous-Style Hymns: Nonbelievers

1. Do nonbelievers you know like the indigenous-style hymns? How do they react to these hymns?

2. Are there any nonbelievers who sing the indigenous-style hymns? Give specific hymns and stories.

3. Have the hymns led nonbelievers to faith in Christ? Give specific situations and stories.

Section III. Evaluation of the Indigenous-Style Hymns

1. Do you like the indigenous-style hymns?

2. Do you prefer slow or fast hymns?

3. What themes do you prefer?

   a. Those that are about God?

   b. Those that are prayers?

   c. Those that praise God?

   d. Other themes?

INTERVIEW RESPONSE SAMPLES

Below are the responses from the ASM congregants in which I present a sampling of the survey results from interview sessions over a two-year period. Because the information collected was large, it is not reasonable to incorporate the corpus that encompasses twenty-five pages of transcribed responses. The reader may access this information through the author. In each instance, the three sections with questions are first listed and then followed by respondent input. Section I, question 2 has two samples. All the others have three.

I displayed the nine hymn titles from the previous round of semi-structured interviews. I then asked the following questions.

Section I: Thoughts about the Indigenous-Style Hymns: Christ Followers

Question 1. Which hymn touches you the most? Why? How?

Sample 1: Respondent 1

I am touched by the hymn "As a Parched Land Thirsts for Water." It is descriptive of how I feel. I get the picture clearly, because I'm from Adana, where it's dry. I remember watering the plants, and they would just soak up the water. In the same way, I see myself as I learn of God and learn of Christ and his work and the Trinity and the wonderful life that we're invited to. I just soak it in, because that is what I need. That is what I'm craving.

Sample 2: Respondent 3

"Pour out Your Spirit on Me" is a hymn that touches me, because I am weak within myself. When God pours out his Spirit, I can live above everything else, all these troubles. I can rise above them, because God's Spirit is being poured on me.

Sample 3: Respondent 11

My favorite hymn is "Cry Out My Heart," because it is what I feel in my heart and I can communicate it to God. It makes me feel very able to connect with God, both what is in my heart out and also carrying me away. I'm very encouraged by this hymn, especially because I'm a quiet person and I don't share much.

Question 2. Which hymns are meaningful to you? Do you have a specific story to tell about these hymns?

Sample 1: Respondent 12

I like "On the Way to Golgotha" very much, because there is great meaning in every word. It makes me feel and imagine a little bit of what Christ walked through.

Sample 2: Respondent 13

Before I came to ASM, I had a dream where I was in this dry land, almost like a desert, and Christ gave me water. So the hymn "In This Desert Called the World" means a lot to me, because it reminds me of that dream. It takes me back there, and the truth of how Christ gives us living water.

Question 3. Are there more hymns that have helped you? Do you have any stories about them?

Sample 1: Respondent 6

The hymn "My Heart Is All about Me" is very truthful. It's like my heart is focused on me, and I pray, "Turn it, O God, turn it away from me!" It reminds me of the evil I have in my life—the ego that just takes over. Vanity, it reminds me of my vanity. Vanity is the worst sin for me, and I have to leave it. Only God can rid me of my sin.

Sample 2: Respondent 8

All these hymns touch me, and I have stories about them, but the deeper thing here is, am I able to receive these messages that God is trying to communicate? Sometimes something rough happens, something difficult happens. These hymns come to my mind, such as "Listen Closely, O My Heart." When I hear this hymn, it makes me stop and consider what God is trying to tell me. What is here? What is happening? It's not just a happening—God is teaching me, and this song reminds me of that.

Sample 3: Respondent 12

I was in Israel for two months last year, and when I was there, I felt very alone because I was away from my family and I could not see them or talk to them as often as usual. So I felt very lonely. The hymn that really touched me was "O Holy River." I asked the Holy Spirit to stay close and to be my comforter. I would sing that song to myself, and I really became one with that hymn and could just sing it all the time. It helped me get through those two months in Israel.

Section II. Thoughts on the Indigenous-Style Hymns: Nonbelievers

Question 1. Do you know nonbelievers who like the indigenous-style hymns? How do they react to these hymns?

Sample 1: Respondent 4

My previous church was more Western. My father was not affected by those hymns, because they were so foreign to him. After I came to this church, he became more interested, asking about God and the idea about the Creator. Because the hymns were in a music style very near to his heart, they became a doorway, a gate for him, an entrance into Christianity, learning more about it. For most Sunni Muslims, their response is like my dad's. If they feel there's something familiar in the church or hymns, then they are drawn to come and see if maybe they can understand. My father likes hearing the *ney* [flute], and that instrument is used in Sufi Islam. When he hears that on Sibel's recordings, it's like "Oh, I know that sound," and then he connects with it. My father realizes that the words are different, but when he hears familiar musical sounds, he listens more carefully.

Sample 2: Respondent 16

I bring my friends here all the time, and when they come in, they suspect that it's going to be different. After a while, they realize there's a part of themselves in the service through these hymns, and it amazes them! We use some of Emre and Mevlana's vocabulary, similar words that we use in the church. When they hear it, they realize, "Wow, part of my culture is here." A lot of evangelical churches use the word *Tanrı* in their hymns. It's the old Turkish word for God versus *Allah*, which is the Arabic word for God. A lot of Muslim Turks use *Allah*, and when they come here and hear us use the word *Allah*, too, they realize that maybe there is more closeness between us than they thought, so they relax. They want to be more involved. Those who are objective come with an open mind. They really appreciate the hymns—they really like them.

Sample 3: Respondent 14

I've had friends who came to this church, and when singing these hymns, they start weeping. They were moved by the songs and the music.

Question 2. Are there any nonbelievers who sing the indigenous-style hymns? Give specific hymns and stories.

Sample 1: Respondent 16

I have a professor friend who came to this church for the Christmas Eve service, where he heard these hymns for the first time, and he still talks about them. I gave the CDs of Turgay's hymns to him. He keeps them in the car, and he's still listening after so many years. He even sings along with the songs. He learned them really fast, and he feels the music as well. Both music and the words are very much a part of us. They're easier for people to remember and sing along

Sample 2: Respondent 7

When nonbelievers come to church, even if it's their first visit, they jump in and start singing. I don't know if they go home and sing these hymns themselves, but when they come here and they are not followers of Jesus, they are able to join in fast and they don't feel they have to simply observe and not participate.

Sample 3: Respondent 6

One of my friends is a Deist, and she is equidistant from all religions, but she does not miss the annual ASM celebrations [Christmas and Easter], when we sing so many of Turgay's hymns. She always comes. She even asks for prayer, and when I go to her house, we sing the songs together.

Sample 4: Respondent 7

I used to sing hymns all the time when I was cooking, and of course, I would sing our Turkish hymns. When I was moving, one of my neighbors said, "We're going to miss your hymns that you sing when you are cooking. We're going to miss those hymns." So I invited them to church where they could hear more of them. They didn't come, but it was really a nice gesture for them to share that.

Question 3. Have the hymns led nonbelievers to faith in Christ? Give some specific situations and stories.

Sample 1: Respondent 14

I really like "Listen Closely, O My Heart," because that was the first hymn that I heard before I became a believer. I came here, and heard about God's sweet voice, his quiet voice that the hymn talks about. When I heard that hymn was written here, it touched me more, knowing that it was local.

Sample 2: Respondent 5

I don't know people who have come to faith through the Turkish hymns, but I know myself. I was just like that. When I first came here, I heard the hymns and I would weep almost every time, and that's when I made a decision that I have to come here. I need to come here. This is where I accepted Christ into my heart. The music is very important, because as Turks we don't have anything in our language where we can talk to the Father Creator, and we don't know how to call out to him, because everything is done in Arabic. Because this is in Turkish, it automatically has a connection within our hearts—that hole we could not fill with Arabic. Now we are able to do it in Turkish, with our language and music, and are able to refer to God as Father, our Creator, in this way.

Sample 3: Respondent 7

There was Mahit *Bey* [Mr. Mahit] who visited our church one Sunday and heard the hymn "My Lord, My Lord, I Give You All My Praise." When he heard that, he started weeping, and he was a Muslim. I reached out and touched him on the shoulder to comfort him, because he was standing right next to me. That's the hymn with which he most connected, and through it, he became a believer. He attended the church until his death.

Section III. Evaluation of the Indigenous-Style Hymns

Question 1. Do you like the indigenous-style hymns?

Sample 1: Respondent 10

I have an Alevi background, so I have similar instruments to what is used in this music and this style of singing. Because of that, I have familiarity with these hymns already, and I feel very close to them.

Sample 2: Respondent 9

These Turkish-style hymns are different from the modern ones. It feels like they are slower and they are deeper. They are deeper in meaning and in what the hymn is trying to say. It might be because of the music, it might be because of the vocabulary, but together, they carry a deeper meaning.

Sample 3: Respondent 1

I remember the first time I heard these hymns. I came in 2010, and I could not believe that something this deep existed in my language. To my Turkish ears, it was deeper than any hymn that I've ever heard. That was very important for me.

Question 2. Do you prefer slow or fast hymns?

Sample 1: Respondent 13

I prefer the slower hymns. To me, they feel deeper, more from the heart.

Sample 2: Respondent 2

I like the slower hymns, because slower hymns are like chewing, eating food. It takes time. As I chew on the words, on the music, on the lyrics, I am encouraged and challenged. It's a process. It's not something fast, and because of that, I feel closer to the slower hymns.

Sample 3: Respondent 1

I do enjoy the slower ones. They really bless me, because I can grasp the meaning better. The music, too, is important for me to hear in these tunes. I grew up listening to it. I heard my father and my grandmother sing this style, so that it really resonates with me, especially some of the instruments, like the *ud* [lute]. The *baglama* [lute] is not in here, but I can easily see it playing along with some of the hymns. I may be imagining the *baglama* working really well, but I also like the *bendir* [Turkish hand drum]. That brings the Sufi, or more mystical, feel to the hymns.

Question 3. What themes do you prefer?

a. Those that are about God?

b. Those that are prayers?

c. Those that praise God?

d. Other themes?

Sample 1, Respondent 10

I like songs filled with love, talking about God's love and all his other characteristics.

Sample 2, Respondent 11

I like the hymns that praise God and talk about his love.

I like the songs that talk about God's power and God's love.

Thank you. This is the end. We have discussed many things. Is there anything else you would like to add to our discussion about the indigenous-style hymns? (There was nothing added).

Glossary

adhan. The Muslim call to worship five times a day, called out by a *muezzin.*

Allāh. The Arabic name for God used by Jews, Christians, and Muslims, including the All Saints Moda assembly.

Alevi, Alevism. Term for a religious, sub-ethnic and cultural people group in Turkey, numbering in the tens of millions. They worship in assembly houses called *cemevi* rather than mosques.

Anatolia. The Asian part of Turkey and one of the first places where Christianity spread. By the fourth century AD, western and central Anatolia was primarily Christian and Greek speaking. It remained so for the following six hundred years.

aqama 'l-salat. Arabic term for "to perform the prayer."

Amida. Jewish traditional "standing" prayer.

arabesk. An Arabic hybrid music genre that was very popular from the 1960s to the 1990s. It melds Turkish classical music and folk elements with those of the West and Egypt. The lyrics are similar in ethos to the blues.

Aşık. An Alevi folk poet/musician.

ayin. The choreographed ceremonial dance-like movements of the Mevlevi Sufi dervishes that preserve the *ayin*'s sacred function, though it is also promoted as a tourist attraction and concert phenomenon.

Bağlama/saz. A lute-like instrument in Turkey that provokes competing claims of ownership from various sectarian groups, including the Alevis ("their sacred instrument"), the Turks ("theirs," based on being the majority population) and the Kurds ("theirs," based on having a longer history in Anatolia than the Turks).

Bar'chu. The Jewish call to worship.

cem. The Alevi closed ceremonial gathering involving poetry, music, and dance.

Glossary

cemevi. An Alevi house of worship.

dede. An Islamic Alevi sociocultural religious leader/teacher in the community.

değiş. Alevi spiritual songs.

dernek or *cemiyet.* Clubs or associations for learning like music, athletics, or languages.

deyiş and *nefes* ("breath"). Poetic songs of mystical love written by Alevi musicians of the fourteenth to twentieth century. The *nefes* are metric, usually with six or nine beats.

dhikr/zikr. Literally, "To remember." Usually refers to the Sufi communal remembrance of the names of God and also designates the entire ritual session for reaching the goal of a mystic experience.

dolmuş. A minibus in Turkey, seating seven to ten people.

du'a, du'aas. Personal prayer (singular and plural spelling).

ezan. Islamic call to prayer.

fasıl. A suite of songs and instrumental pieces in Ottoman classical music, played continuously without interludes and interconnected through improvisation

halāl. Lawful or permissible for use by Muslims.

halk music. Folk music.

harām. Forbidden for use by Muslims.

ilahi. "For God," a general Turkish phrase applied to sung prayers.

imam. Worship leader of mosque.

Istanbulite(s). A resident (or residents) of Istanbul.

kanun. A Turkish zither-like musical instrument.

Mevlevi. A member of the Mevlevi Sufi Order (followers of Mevlana Jelaleddin Rumi) or "Whirling Dervishes," which was founded by Rumi's son.

mevlut (or mevlit). Musical settings of the birth of the Prophet Muhammad.

mosque. A Muslim place of worship.

muezzin. A man who calls Muslims to prayer five times a day from the minaret in a mosque.

mufti. A Sunni Islamic scholar who interprets or expounds Islamic law.

munajats. Texts that glorify Allah.

musiqa ("music"). A lower-level category of musical expression in Muslim countries that combines pitch and rhythm, normally classified as "music" in Western culture.

nafs. Considered to be the "lower passions" of an individual.

ney. A Turkish flute.

non-musiqa ("non-music"). A higher-level category of musical expression in Muslim countries that combines pitch and rhythm, normally classified as "music" in Western culture. All genres of *non-musiqa*, including the call to prayer, recitation of the Qur'an as well as chanted poetry are considered *halal*.

Oud (ûd, Arabic). This is a pear-shaped stringed instrument with eleven or twelve strings in five or six courses. Commonly used throughout the Middle East, its construction is similar to a lute.

oyun havas. A dance tune signature to Roma (gypsy) weddings in Turkey.

qur'anic cantillation. Recitation of the Qur'an in a tonal manner.

Roma. An ethnic term for gypsies, a group of people who maintain a nomadic way of life.

sama. This generally refers to the whirling in a Mevlevi Sufi ceremony, while *mukābala* is the entire "hearing" occasion, including the recitation of the Qur'an and the poetry of Rumi. *Devr*, or *Sultan Veled Devri*, refers to the circular movements of dervishes around the *sama* hall three times during the *mukābala*.

saalat. Muslim obligatory ritual prayer five times a day.

saalla. Islamic word for "to bow" used for institutionalized prayer. It was used for corporate prayer in synagogues and churches long before Muhammad.

Saama hane. Refers to the large room or Sufi lodge where the *sama* ceremony is performed.

Sanat music. Turkish art music after 1923. Still popular today.

şarkı. An urban art-music form that originated in the 1600s within the Ottoman Empire and is considered to be a national song form that captures the emotional life of the Turks in modern Turkish, *şarkı* is the common word for any song.

saemah. The Alevi ceremonial dance performed in *cems*.

Sheikh. Sufi spiritual leader.

Shiite, Shia. The second largest branch of Islam in Turkey.

siddur. A Jewish prayer book, containing a set order of daily prayers.

Sufi. A Muslim ascetic and mystic.

Sufism (Taşawwuf). Refers to the mystical branches of Islam that developed alongside the Orthodox branch and involves ecstatic rituals of worship.

Sunni. The larger of the two main branches of Islam and adheres to the Orthodox tradition that acknowledges the first four caliphs as rightful successors of Mohammad. It also stresses the importance of Sunni as a basis for law.

tarakat. A religious Sufi brotherhood.

tekkes. Sufi houses of worship.

Türk sanat müziği. A term for Turkish classic music, the musical genre preference of urbanites, the upper class, and sultan's palaces. The Turkish music system of this genre is based upon modal patterns (*makamlar*) ruled by composition rules different from Western music.

Glossary

türkü. The word for "Turkish-language only" folk songs collected from every province in Turkey. Those originally in other languages were either translated on the spot by folklorists or translated at a later time in Ankara.

ummah. An Arabic word for the lay members of the supranational Sunni Islamic community.

yeşil ("green") pop. Muslim religious pop-style music.

zikr/dhikr. Means the same as *dhikr/zikr* above, "to remember."

Index of Song Lyric Examples

Bibliography

Akkaya, Ayhan, and Fehmiye Çelik, eds. *60'lardan 70'lere 45'lik arkılar* [45 rpm song singles from the 60s to the 70s]. Istanbul: BGST Yayınları, 2006.

Avery, Tom. "Music of the Heart: The Power of Indigenous Worship in Reaching Unreached Peoples with the Gospel." *Mission Frontiers* 18 (1996) 13–14.

Aydemir, Murat. *Turkish Music Makam Guide*. Edited and translated by Erman Dirikcan. Istanbul: Pan Yayıncılık, 2010.

Aytar, Volkan, and Azer Keskin. "Construction of Spaces of Music in Istanbul: Scuffling and Intermingling Sounds in a Fragmented Metropolis." In *Géocarrefour* 78 (2003) 147–58.

Balisky, Lila W. "Songs of Ethiopia's Tesfaye Gabbiso: Singing with Understanding in Babylon, the Meantime and Zion." DMiss diss., Fuller Theological Seminary, 2015.

———. *Songs of Ethiopia's Tesfaye Gabbiso: Singing with Understanding in Babylon, the Meantime, and Zion*. American Society of Missiology Monograph Series 37. Eugene, OR: Pickwick, 2018.

Barnett, Jens. "Refusing to Choose: Multiple Belonging among Arab Followers of Christ." In *Longing for Community*, edited by David Greenlee. Pasadena, CA: William Carey Library, 2013.

Barz, Gregory F. *Performing Religion: Negotiating Past and Present in Kwaya Music of Tanzania*. Amsterdam: Rodopi, 2003.

Bates, Eliot. *Music in Turkey: Experiencing Music, Expressing Culture*. Oxford: Oxford University Press, 2011.

Béhague, Gerald, ed. *Performance Practice: Ethnomusicological Perspectives*. Westport: Greenwood, 1984.

Bell, Catherine. *Ritual Theory, Ritual Practice*. New York: Oxford University Press, 1992.

Bell, Judith. *Doing Your Research Project*. 5th ed. Maidenhead: Open University Press, 2010.

Bernard, H. Russell. *Social Research Methods: Qualitative and Quantitative Approaches*. Thousand Oaks, CA: Sage, 2000.

Bevans, Stephen B. *Models of Contextual Theology*. Rev. ed. Maryknoll, NY: Orbis, 2012.

Bibliography

Bevans, Stephen B., and Roger Schroeder. *Constants in Context: A Theology of Mission for Today*. Maryknoll, New York: Orbis, 2004.

Bloom, Benjamin S., *Taxonomy of Educational Objectives*. Boston: Allyn and Bacon, 1956.

Bourdieu, Pierre. *The Logic of Practice*. Translated by Richard Nice. Stanford: Stanford University Press, 1980.

Brislen, Mike. "A Model for a Muslim-Culture Church." In *Missiology: An International Review* 24 (1996) 353–67.

Brown, Rupert. "Social Identity Theory: Past Achievements, Current Problems and Future Challenges." In *European Journal of Social Psychology* 30 (2000) 745–78.

Bullinger, E. W. *Figures of Speech Used in the Bible: Explained and Illustrated*. Baltimore: Delmarva, 1898.

Bultema, James. "Muslims Coming to Christ in Turkey." In *International Journal of Frontier Missiology* 27 (2010) 27–31.

Bulut, Uzay. "Churches in Turkey on the Verge of Extinction." In *Gatestone Institute*, April 19, 2015. http://www.gatestoneinstitute.org/5584/turkey-churches.

Caballero, Lorraine. "Christian Presence Key to Mideast Stability, Iraqi Leaders Tell UN." In *Christian Daily*, December 2, 2017. https://www.christiandaily.com/article/christian-presence-key-to-mideast-stability-iraqi leaders-tell-un/61572.html.

Carnes, Tony. "Jesus in Turkey." In *Christianity Today*, January 1, 2008. https://www.christianitytoday.com/ct/2008/january/12.25.html.

Chapman, Deborah Herath. "Florencio Segura: Communicating Quechua Evangelical Theology Vie Hymnody in Southern Peru." PhD diss., University of Edinburgh, 2006.

Chastain, Mary. "Endangered Species: Christianity at the Brink of Extinction in Turkey." *Breitbart News Network*, April 21, 2015. http://www.breitbart.com/national-security/2015/04/21/endangered-species-christianity-at-the-brink-of-extinction-in-turkey.

Chenoweth, Vida. "Part 3: Peoples of Oceania and Their Music, Irian Jaya Province of Indonesia." In *Garland Encyclopedia of World Music Volume 9: Australia and the Pacific Islands)*. Edited by Adrienne L. Kaeppler and J.W. Love. New York: Taylor & Francis Group, 1998.

———. "Spare Them Western Music!" In *Missio Nexus: Learn, Meet, Engage in the Great Commission*, January 1, 1984. https://missionexus.org/spare-them-western-music/.

Chenoweth, Vida, and Darlene Bee. "On Ethnic Music." In *Practical Anthropology* 15 (1968) 205–12.

Cherry, Constance. *The Worship Architect*. Grand Rapids: Baker, 2010.

Central Intelligence Agency. "Turkey." https://www.cia.gov/the-world-factbook/countries/turkey/.

"City Population. Istanbul (Turkey): Districts, Cities, Towns, and Villages." https://www.citypopulation.de/en/turkey/istanbul/.

Chupungco, Anscar. "Liturgical Inculturation: The Future That Awaits Us." In *Institute of Liturgical Studies Occasional Papers* 96:248–60, 2003. https://scholar.valpo.edu/ils_papers/96.

———. *Liturgical Inculturation: Sacramentals, Religiosity, and Catechesis*. Collegeville, MN: Liturgical, 1992.

Ciabattari, Jane. "Why is Rumi the Best-Selling Poet in the US?" *BBC News*, Oct 21, 2014. http://www.bbc.com/culture/story/20140414-americas-best-selling-poet, 2014.

Clark, Douglas F. "Turkish Halk Worship Music: The Muslim Background Believer Churches of Turkey at Worship in the Language of Their Own People." PhD diss., Evangel University, 2014.

Cohen, Louis, and Lawrence Manion. *Research Methods in Education.* 4th ed. London: Routledge, 1994.

Corbitt, J. Nathan. *The Sound of the Harvest: Music in Global Christianity.* Grand Rapids: Baker, 1998.

Craigie, Peter C. *Psalms 1–50.* Word Biblical Commentary 19. Waco, TX: Word, 1983.

Crainshaw, Jill Y. *Wise and Discerning Hearts: An Introduction to Wisdom Liturgical Theology.* Collegeville, MN: Liturgical, 2000.

Creswell, John W. *Qualitative Inquiry and Research Design: Choosing Among Five Traditions.* Thousand Oaks, CA: Sage, 2012.

D'Andrade, Roy. *The Development of Cognitive Anthropology.* Cambridge: Cambridge University Press, 1995.

Değirmenci, Koray. *Creating Global Music in Turkey.* Lanham, MD: Lexington. 2013.

Denzin, Norman K. *Interpretive Interactionism.* Newbury Park, CA: Sage, 1989.

Dogan, Ali. "Turkey: The Alevi Faith, Principles, Beliefs, Rituals and Practices (1995–2005)." *Hurriyet Daily News,* October 1, 2004. https://www.refworld.org/docid/42df61b320.html.

Donin, Hayim Halevy. *To Pray as a Jew: A Guide to the Prayer Book and the Synagogue Service.* New York: Basic, 1991.

Dyer, Jeff, etl al. *The Innovator's DNA: Mastering the Five Skills of Disruptive Innovators.* Boston: Harvard Business Press, 2011.

Engel, James. *Contemporary Christian Communications: Its Theory and Practice.* Nashville: Thomas Nelson, 1979.

Faroe, Charles E. "Questioning Belonging: Some Issues of Identity and Belonging for MBBs in Turkey." Unpublished paper, PhD student at IBTSC/VU University in Amsterdam, 2018.

Feldman, Zev. "Ottoman Music." In *Oxford Music Online/Grove Music Online.* https://www.oxfordmusiconline.com/grovemusic/view/10.1093/gmo/9781561592630.001.0001/omo-9781561592630-e-0000052169.

Fiske, John. *Understanding Popular Culture.* New York: Routledge, 1994.

Fowler, James. *Weaving the New Creation: Stages of Faith and the Public Church.* New York: Harper Collins, 1991.

Frith, Simon. "Introduction." In *World Music, Politics and Social Change: Papers from the International Association for the Study of Popular Music.* Edited by Simon Frith. New York: St. Martin's Press, 1989.

Fromkin, David. *A Peace to End All Peace: The Fall of the Ottoman Empire and the Creation of the Modern Middle East.* New York: Henry Hold and Company, 1989.

Green, Tim. "Conversion in the Light of Identity Theories." In *Longing for Community,* edited by David Greenlee. Pasadena, CA: William Carey Library, 2013.

Greve, Martin. *Makamsız: Individualization of Traditional Music on the Eve of Kemalist Turkey.* Würzburg: Ergon Verlag Würzburg in Kommission, 2017.

Grimes, Ronald L. *Beginnings in Ritual Studies.* 3rd ed. Waterloo, Canada: Ritual Studies International, 2010.

Güvenç, Bozkurt. "We Turks." In *Türk kimşiği.* Istanbul, Turkey: Boyut, 1993.

Hartnell, Malcolm. "Oral Contextualization: Communicating Biblical Truth to the Digo of Kenya." PhD diss., Fuller Theological Seminary, 2009.

Hawn, C. Michael. *Gather into One: Praying and Singing Globally.* Grand Rapids: Eerdmans, 2003.

Bibliography

Heredia, Rudolf C. *Changing Gods: Rethinking Conversion in India*. London: Penguin, 2007.

Hiebert, Paul G. *Anthropological Insights for Missionaries*. Grand Rapids: Baker, 1985.

————. *Anthropological Reflections on Missiological Issues*. Grand Rapids: Baker, 1994.

————. "Critical Contextualization," In *International Bulletin of Missionary Research* 11 (1987) 104–12.

————. "Form and Meaning in Contextualization of the Gospel." In *Word Among Us*, edited by Dean S. Gilliland, 101–20. Dallas: Word, 1989.

Hiebert, Paul G., et al. *Understanding Folk Religion: Christian Response to Popular Beliefs and Practices*. Grand Rapids: Baker, 1999.

Holt, Peter, et al., eds. *The Cambridge History of Islam* 2B. Cambridge: Cambridge University Press, 2000.

Hood, Mantle. "The Challenge of 'Bi-Musicality.'" In *Ethnomusicology* 4 (1960) 55–59, 1960.

Huntington, Samuel P. "The Clash of Civilizations." In *Foreign Affairs* 72 (1993) 22.

Hürriyet Daily News. "Istanbul One of Four Anchor Megacities of Europe: Research." http://www.hurriyetdailynews.com/istanbul-one-of-four-anchor-megacities-of-europe-research.aspx?pageID=238&nid=92496&NewsCatID=345, 2015.

Hustad, Donald. *Jubilate! Church Music in the Evangelical Tradition*. Carol Stream, IL: Hope, 1981.

Huyser-Honig, Joan. "Ethnodoxology: Calling all Peoples to Worship in their Heart Language." Calvin Institute of Christian Worship, Feb 10, 2009. https://worship.calvin.edu/resources/resource-library/ethnodoxology-calling-all-peoples-to-worship-in-their-heart-language/.

Jennings, Theodore W. "On Ritual Knowledge." In *Journal of Religion* 62 (1982) 111–27.

Johnson, Samuel. Letter to Hester Thrale (Sept 21, 1773). https://thrale.com/parting_letters_hester_thrale_and_samuel_johnson.

Jones, Lang Lasalle. "Istanbul Among Top Four Megacities of Europe." https://www.istanbulview.com/istanbul/news/.

Jorgensen, D. L. *Participant Observation: A Methodology for Human Studies*. Newbury Park, CA: Sage, 1989.

Kandiyoti, Deniz, and Ayşe Saktanber, eds. *Fragments of Culture: The Everyday of Modern Turkey*. New Brunswick, NJ: Rutgers University Press, 2002.

Kavanagh, Aidan. *On Liturgical Theology*. Collegeville, MN: Liturgical, 1984.

Keating, Ryan. "The State of the Turkish Church," email. July 31, 2014.

Keyder, Çağlar, ed. *Istanbul: Between the Global and the Local*. Lanham, MD: Rowman and Littlefield, 1999.

Kimberlin, Cynthia Tse. "The Scholarship and Art of Ashenafi Kebede (1938-1998)." In *Ethnomusicology* 43 (1999) 322–34.

King, Roberta R. *Music in the Life of the African Church*. Waco, TX: Baylor University Press, 2008.

————. "Pathways in Christian Music Communication: The Case of the Senufu of Côte d'Ivoire." PhD diss., Fuller Theological Seminary, 1989.

————. *Pathways in Christian Music Communication: The Case of the Senufo of Côte d'Ivoire*. American Society of Missiology Monograph Series 3. Eugene, OR: Pickwick, 2009.

Klaser, Rajna. "From an Imagined Paradise to an Imagined Nation: Interpreting Şarkı as a Cultural Play." PhD diss., University of California, Berkeley, 2001.

Krabill, James R. "Encounters: What Happens to Music When People Meet." In *Music in the Life of the African Church*, edited by Roberta R. King, 57–79. Waco: Baylor University Press, 2008.

Kraft, Charles H. *Christianity in Culture: A Study in Biblical Theologizing in Cross-Cultural Perspective.* Revised 25th anniversary ed. Maryknoll, NY: Orbis, 2005.

Laitman, Rav Michael. *Basic Concepts in Kabbalah.* Brooklyn: Laitman Kabbalah, 2006.

Lasley, Thomas J., II. "Bloom's Taxonomy." *Encyclopaedia Britannica.* https://www.brit annica.com/topic/Blooms-taxonomy.

Lathrop, Gordon. *Holy Things: A Liturgical Theology.* Minneapolis: Fortress, 1993.

Levias, Caspar, ed. "Numbers and Numerals." http://www.jewishencyclopedia.com/articles /11619-numbers-and-numerals.

Loh, I-to, ed. *Sound the Bamboo.* Chicago: GIA, 2000.

Lotrecchiano, Gaetano R. "Ethnomusicology and the Study of Musical Change." In *Liturgical Ministry* 6 (1997) 108–19.

Luzbetak, Louis J. *The Church and Cultures: An Applied Anthropology for the Religious Worker.* Techny, IL: Divine Word, 1963.

Lynch, Marc. "How Muslims really think about Islam." In *Foreign Policy.* https://foreign policy.com/2012/08/09/how-muslims-really-think-about-islam/.

Magesa, Laurenti. *Anatomy of Inculturation: Transforming the Church in Africa.* Maryknoll, NY: Orbis, 2004.

Malina, Bruce J. *The New Testament World: Insights from Cultural Anthropology.* Rev. ed. Louisville: Westminster John Knox, 1993.

Markoff, Irene. "Introduction to Sufi Music and Ritual in Turkey." In *Middle East Studies Association Bulletin* 29 (1995) 157–60.

McGann, Mary E. *Exploring Music as Worship and Theology: Research in Liturgical Practice.* Collegeville, MN: The Order of St. Benedict, 2002.

———. "Interpreting the Ritual Role of Music in Christian Liturgical Practice." PhD diss., Berkeley: Graduate Theological Union, 1996.

Merriam, Alan P. *The Anthropology of Music.* Evanston, IL: Northwestern University Press, 1964.

Moreau, A. Scott. *Contextualization in World Missions: Mapping and Assessing Evangelical Models.* Grand Rapid: Kregel, 2012.

Nettl, Bruno. "The Harmless Drudge: Defining Ethnomusicology." In *The Study of Ethnomusicology: Thirty-One Issues and Concepts,* 3–15. Chicago: University of Illinois Press, 2005.

Nicholls, Ruth. "Catechisms and Chants: A Case for Using Liturgies in Ministry to Muslims." DMin diss., Australian College of Theology, 2008.

Öncü, Ayşe. "Istanbulites and Others: The Cultural Cosmology of Being Middle Class in the Era of Globalism." In *Istanbul: Between the Global and the Local,* edited by Çaglar Keyder, 95–121. Lanham, MD: Rowman and Littlefield, 1999.

Öztüna, Yılmaz. *Büyük Türk Müsik Mûsikîsi Ansiklopedisi/Great Encyclopedia of Turkish Music* 2. Ankara: Kültür Bakanlığı, 1990.

Ozturk, Yasar Nuri. *The Eye of the Heart: An Introduction to Sufism and the Major Tariqats of Anatolia and the Balkans.* Translated by Richard Blakney. Istanbul: Redhouse, 1988.

Padwick, Constance E. *Muslim Devotions: A Study of Prayer-Manuals in Common Use.* Oxford: Oneworld, 2003.

Bibliography

Papas, Alexandre. "Toward a New History of Sufism: The Turkish Case." *History of Religions* 46 (2006) 81–90.

Parshall, Phil, ed. *The Last Great Frontier: Essays on Muslim Evangelism.* Quezon City, Philippines: Open Doors with Brother Andrew, 2000.

Perigo, Jeremy. "Leading a Workshop on Contextual Songwriting for Worship Musicians at Burn 24–7 Middle East." Doctor of Worship Studies diss., Robert E. Webber Institute for Worship Studies, 2013.

Perrin, Cathy, and Wayne Perrin. "When I Look into Your Holiness." Capitol CMG Publishing, 1981.

Pikkert, Peter. "Protestant Missionaries to the Middle East: Ambassadors of Christ or Culture?" PhD diss., University of South Africa, 2006.

Qureshi, Regula. *Sufi Music of India and Pakistan.* Cambridge: Cambridge University Press, 1987.

Reinhard, Kurt, and Martin Stokes. "Turkey II, Folk Music." *Oxford Music Online /Grove Music Online.* http://www.oxfordmusiconline.com/grovemusic/.

———. "Turkey IV: Art Music." In *Oxford Music Online/Grove Music Online*, 9–19. http://www.oxfordmusiconline.com/grovemusic/.

———. "Turkey V: Popular Music." In *Oxford Music Online/Grove Music Online*, 19–22. http://www.oxfordmusiconline.com/grovemusic/.

Rimmer, Mark. "Songs in the Key of Life: The Musical Habitus and Young People' Community Music Participation." PhD diss., University of Newcastle Upon Tyne, 2006.

Routley, Erik. *Hymns and Human Life.* Grand Rapids: Eerdmans, 1959.

Saktanber, Ayşe. "'We Pray Like You Have Fun:' New Islamic Youth in Turkey between Intellectualism and Popular Culture." In *Fragments of Culture: The Everyday of Modern Turkey*, edited by Kandiyoti, Deniz and Ayşe Saktanber, 254–76. New Brunswick, NJ: Rutgers University Press, 2002.

Savas, Bulent, "Example 1: Accidentals of Turkish Classical Music." http://www.bulent savas.com/english/althtml/whatare.htm.

Schrag, Brian, and James R. Krabill. *Creating Local Arts Together: A Manual to Help Communities Reach Their Kingdom Goals.* Pasadena, CA: William Carey Library, 2013.

Schreiter, Robert. *Constructing Local Theologies.* London: Orbis, 2006.

Schwartz, Steven. "How Many Sufis Are There in Islam?" https://www.huffpost.com/ entry/how-many-sufis-in-world-i_b_902164.

Şentürk, Rıdvan. "Turgay Üçal." In *Müzik Kimlik*, 411–21. Istanbul: Küre Yayınları, 2016.

Shelemay, Kay Kaufman. *The Ethnomusicologist and the Transmission of Tradition.* Oakland, CA: UC Press, 1996.

Shenk, Wilbert R. *Changing Frontiers of Mission.* Maryknoll, NY: Orbis, 1999.

Sherinian, Zoe. "The Indigenization of Tamil Christian Music: Folk Music as a Liberative transmission system Theology." PhD diss., Wesleyan University, 1998.

Shorter, Aylward. *Toward a Theology of Inculturation.* Eugene, OR: Orbis, 2006.

Shubin, Russell G. "Worship That Moves the Soul: A Conversation with Roberta King." In *Mission Frontiers* 23 (2001) 10–15.

Signell, Karl L. *Makam: Modal Practice in Turkish Art Music.* Sarasota, FL: Usul, 2008.

Smith, Donald K. *Creating Understanding: A Handbook for Christian Communication across Cultural Landscapes.* Grand Rapids: Zondervan, 1992.

Spradley, James P. *Participant Observation.* Fort Worth: Harcourt Brace College, 1980.

Stetzer, Ed. "Avoiding the Pitfall of Syncretism." In *Christianity Today*, July 15, 2014. https://www.christianitytoday.com/edstetzer/2014/june/avoiding-pitfall-of-syncretism.html.

Stokes, Martin. "Music." In *The Routledge Handbook of Modern Turkey*, edited by Metin Heper and Sabri Sayarı, 96–106. New York: Routledge, 2012.

———. *The Republic of Love: Cultural Intimacy in Turkish Popular Music*. Chicago: University of Chicago Press, 2004.

———. "Republic of Turkey." In *The New Grove Dictionary of Music and Musicians*, edited by Stanley Sadie and John Tyrrell, 19:168–78. New York: Macmillan, 2004.

———. "Turkey II: Folk Music." In *Oxford Music Online/Grove Music Online*, 2–8. http://www.oxfordmusiconline.com/grovemusic/.

Stone, Ruth. *Let the Inside Be Sweet: The Interpretation of Music Event among the Kpelle of Liberia*. Bloomington: Indiana University Press, 1982.

Tippett, Alan Richard. *Solomon Islands Christianity*. Pasadena, CA: William Carey Library, 1967.

Titon, Jeff Todd, ed. *Worlds of Music: An Introduction to the Music of the World's Peoples*. Boston: Schirmer, 2002.

Toksöz, Itir. "Orchestrating Multiple Eastern-Western Identities through Music: A Turkish Story." In *Music and Solidarity: Questions of Universality, Consciousness, and Connection*, edited by Felicity Laurence and Oliver Urbain, 83–99. New Brunswick, NJ: Transaction, 2011.

"Today in Istanbul." https://www.frommers.com/destinations/istanbul/in-depth/today.

Tovey, Phillip. *Inculturation of Christian Worship: Exploring the Eucharist*. Burlington, VT: Ashgate, 2004.

Üçal, Turgay. *Dönün Rab'binize* (Return to Your Lord). Sibel Üçal, soloist. Istanbul, Turkey: Istanbul Presbiteryen Kilisesi, 1998.

———. "From Church Planting to Human Planting." Unpublished article, 2016.

———. *Haykır Yüreğim* (Cry Out, My Heart), CD double disk (Turkish and English-languages). Istanbul, Turkey: Mega Müzik, 2014.

———. *Haykır Yüreğim* (Cry Out, My Heart). Sibel Üçal, soloist. Music videos. Istanbul, Turkey: All Saints Moda. https://www.youtube.com/watch?v=z3VMEsafR2w&list=PLQfi14V3hHoJDV-udY1X7ac8DfTQyVJcI.

———. *İsevi-Sufi Geleneği Hristiyan Türk ilahileri* (Almighty: New Turkish Christian Hymns in the Sufi Tradition). Sibel Üçal, soloist. Istanbul, Turkey: Metropol, 2005.

———. *İsevi-Sufi Geleneği Hristiyan Türk ilahileri* (Created to Give Glory: New Turkish Christian Hymns in the Sufi Tradition). Sibel Üçal, soloist. Istanbul, Turkey: Metropol, 2005.

———. "Şabat Ayini *İlahiler*" (Sabbath Ritual Hymns). Istanbul, 2005.

———. *Şabat Ayini-Serifi* (Sabbath Rite). Istanbul, Turkey: All Saints Moda, 2007.

———. *Sofraya Yaklaşırken* (Approaching the Table). Istanbul, Turkey: All Saints Moda, 2008.

———. *Vakit İbadeti* (Daily Worship). Istanbul: GDK, 2013.

———. *Vakit İbadeti* (Daily Worship). Istanbul: GDK, 2014.

———. *Vakit İbadeti* (Daily Worship). Istanbul: GDK, 2015.

———. *Varlığının Sakinliğinde* (The Tranquility of the Existence). Sibel Üçal and Gülmira Başaran, vocalists. Istanbul, Turkey: All Saints Moda, 2006

Bibliography

Vincent, Ntrie-Akpabi. "Inculturation as Self-Identification: An African in Search of Authentic Christian Identity. A Theological Enquiry Among the Ewe of Ghana." Master's diss., Universidade Catolica Portuguesa Faculdade de Teologia, 2016.

Wallace, Cory. "Devastation in Turkey: The Church Responds." In *Mission Frontiers* (January 1, 2000).

Walter, Howard A. "Missionary Qualifications." In *International Review of Missions*, October 1, 1921. https://onlinelibrary.wiley.com/doi/abs/10.1111/j.1758–e6631.1921.tb04610.x.

Watts, Michael J. "Mapping Meaning, Denoting Difference, Imagining Identity: Dialectical Images and Postmodern Geographies." In *Geografiska Annaler: Series B, Human Geography* 73 (1991) 7–16.

Westerhoff, J. "Liturgy and Catechetics." In *Worship* 61 (1987) 510–16.

White, Jennie. *Muslim Nationalism and the New Turks*. Princeton: Princeton University Press, 2013.

Willms, Dennis G., et al. "A Systematic Approach for Using Qualitative Method in Primary Prevention Research." In *Medical Anthropology Quarterly* 4 (1990) 391–409.

Wilson, Pam. "Striving Together for the Faith of the Gospel: A United Approach to Mission in Turkey 1961–1996." Class paper. Fuller Seminary (1996) 5.

Witvliet, John D. "Theological and Conceptual Models for Liturgy and Culture." In *Liturgy Digest* 3 (1996) 5–46.

Wolper, Ethel Sara. *Cities and Saints: Sufism and the Transformation of Urban Space in Medieval Anatolia*. University Park, PA: Pennsylvania State University Press, 2003.

WorldAtlas. "Major Religions in Turkey." https://www.worldatlas.com/articles/religious-beliefs-in-turkey.html.

Yeşilçay, Mehmet Cemal. *One God: Psalms and Hymns from Orient and Occident*. Pera Ensemble Istanbul. Switzerland: Ludi Musici LM 003, 2009.

Yin, Robert K. *Case Study Research: Design and Methods: Applied Social Research Methods*. Thousand Oaks, CA: Sage, 2009.

Zubaida, Sami. "Turkish Islam and National Identity." In *Middle East Report* 199 (1996) 2015.

Zürcher, Erik J. *Turkey: A Modern History*. New York: I. B. Tauris, 2001.

Index

Index

Index

Index

Index